PRAISE FOR RUTH GRUBER'S

VIRGINIA WOOLF: THE WILL TO CREATE AS A WOMAN, from a leading scholar of Virginia Woolf's life and work

"The recovery of this brilliant book demands an instant rewriting of literary history. For now we know that Virginia Woolf's work found the critic she deserved in a 19-year-old Brooklyn Jewish girl's Ph.D. at Cologne University in 1931. Little is to be found among the hundreds of biographies and critical studies of Virginia Woolf that can match the insights of this perceptive book. For Ruth Gruber was the first to recognize the driving ambition of Virginia Woolf to be "Shakespearianna," to compete with and surpass the whole of British literary history. Ruth Gruber discovers and explicates Woolf's feminist will to power, her desire to write ruthlessly as a woman and only as a woman, whatever that might mean to her literary practice. Gruber's work is a masterpiece of feminist criticism to be put on the shelf next to *A Room of One's Own*."

Jane Marcus
Distinguished Professor of English
CUNY Graduate Center and the
City College of New York

VIRGINIA WOOLF

The Will to Create as a Woman

RUTH GRUBER

VIRGINIA WOOLF: A STUDY,
beginning on page 55, is a facsimile reproduction
of the original 1935 edition of the work.

CARROLL & GRAF PUBLISHERS
NEW YORK

VIRGINIA WOOLF
The Will to Create as a Woman

Carroll & Graf Publishers
An Imprint of Avalon Publishing Group Inc.
245 West 17th Street
11th Floor
New York, NY 10011

AVALON
publishing group incorporated

First Carroll & Graf edition 2005

Essay originally published in 1935 as *Virginia Woolf: A Study*
by Verlag von Bernhard Tauchnitz in Leipzig, Germany.

Library of Congress Cataloging-in-Publication Data is available.

ISBN: 0-7867-1534-0

9 8 7 6 5 4 3 2

Printed in the United States of America
Distributed by Publishers Group West

To my grandchildren
Michael Evans and Lucy Evans
&
Joel Michaels and Lila Michaels:
Four votes of confidence in our future

CONTENTS

INTRODUCTION
    My Hours with Virginia Woolf   1

HISTORICAL DOCUMENTS   37
    Letter from Peggy Belsher of Hogarth Press
        to Ruth Gruber, Dec. 16, 1931   39
    Letter of Recommendation from Barnes & Noble
        editor A. W. Littlefield, Feb. 25, 1933   40
    Letter from Ruth Gruber to Virginia Woolf,
        May 8, 1935   41
    Letter from M. West of Hogarth Press
        to Ruth Gruber, May 17, 1935   42
    Letter from Ruth Gruber to M. West
        of Hogarth Press, May 28, 1935   43
    Letter from Virginia Woolf to Ruth Gruber,
        June 21, 1935   44
    Letter from Virginia Woolf to Ruth Gruber,
        Oct. 12, 1935   45
    Letter from Ruth Gruber to Virginia Woolf,
        Dec. 27, 1935   46
    Letter from Virginia Woolf to Ruth Gruber,
        Jan. 10, 1936   47
    Promotional booklet for lecture bureau
        representing Dr. Ruth Gruber   48–51

Letter from Nigel Nicolson to Aïda Lovell
    (for Ruth Gruber), Aug. 31, 1989   52
Letter from Ruth Gruber to Nigel Nicolson,
    Sept. 15, 1989   53
Letter from Nigel Nicolson to Ruth Gruber,
    Sept. 25, 1989   54

VIRGINIA WOOLF: A STUDY
    by Ruth Gruber, originally published in 1935   55
    Chapter One—The Poet versus the Critic   61
    Chapter Two—The Struggle for a Style   69
    Chapter Three—Literary Influences: The Formation
        of a Style   84
    Chapter Four—The Style Completed and the Thought
        Implied   99
    Chapter Five—"The Waves"—the Rhythm of Conflicts   124
    Chapter Six—The Will to Create as a Woman   138

A MYSTERY SOLVED   161

INDEX   169

ABOUT THE AUTHOR   175

INTRODUCTION

MY HOURS WITH
VIRGINIA WOOLF

MY HOURS WITH VIRGINIA WOOLF

One morning in the summer of 2004, my research assistant, Maressa Gershowitz, came running into the room where I was working.

"Look what I've found!" she shouted.

She held up three letters, sent to me by Virginia Woolf.

The letters were as fresh and unwrinkled as if Woolf had written them not in 1935 and 1936, but the day before.

"Where in heaven's name did you find these letters?"

"You won't believe this," Maressa said. "They were in the back of one of your filing cabinets, behind a bunch of old tax returns."

The past lit up. I shut my eyes, recalling how in 1931–32, as an American exchange student at the University of Cologne in Germany, I had written my doctoral thesis, called "Virginia Woolf: A Study." Three years later, it was published as a paperback book in Leipzig under the same title. With apprehension, I had sent Woolf the book, and she had invited me to her London home for tea.

I recalled how on that day, the fifteenth day of October, 1935, I had walked up and down the narrow streets of Bloomsbury. I stared up at Virginia Woolf's Georgian four-story house, which had a balcony overhanging the street.

Everything seemed magical to me. The rain, which had fallen all day, had stopped, and the air was as clean as if it had been scrubbed in a huge washing machine.

I rang the bell at 6 P.M. at 52 Tavistock Square. A housekeeper in a black-and-white uniform opened the door, led me into a dark corridor and up a narrow staircase to the first floor. She tapped on a wooden door, and a man who introduced himself as Leonard Woolf stepped forward.

"Welcome," he spoke warmly and shook my hand. He was painfully thin, with a long oval face, dark hooded eyes, black hair laced with gray, and an air of sadness and suffering. He took me across a large parlor with sofas on each side, and motioned me to sit in an upholstered armchair close to Virginia.

She lay stretched out in front of a fireplace. The fire cast a glow over her carved straight nose, her expressive lips, her melancholy gray-green eyes. The beautiful Nicole Kidman, playing her in the film *The Hours*, did not need the built-up nose or the dowdy housewife clothes. Virginia Woof was elegant, a woman of grace and beauty.

She was a study in gray: short gray hair cut like a boy's, a flowing ankle-length gray gown, gray shoes, and gray stockings. In her fingers, she held a long silver cigarette holder, through which she blew smoke into the parlor. There were three of us: Virginia, then fifty-three, reclining on a rug; her husband Leonard behind me, at the far end of the room but leaning forward as if he were hovering over her; and I, sitting inches away from her. I had come to sit at her feet. But now she was lying at mine.

The fire warmed me in front as I faced her, but my back was chilled. I pulled my jacket tight around me and sat in silence, too overawed to speak.

"I looked into the study you wrote about me," she said. "Quite scholarly."

Was she praising me? I could scarcely believe it. I did not know whether to thank her or remain silent. I chose silence.

She took a long draft of smoke and said, "I understand from my secretary that you are writing a book on women under fascism, communism, and democracy."

I murmured, "Yes."

"And you want to interview me for your book. I don't know how I can help you. I don't understand a thing about politics. I never worked a day in my life."

I wondered how she considered that it was not work to write groundbreaking novels, brilliant essays, and book reviews, and why she would demean her knowledge of politics. Her books were full of politics; her friends in the Bloomsbury crowd were energetic political thinkers—Lytton Strachey, the poet and historian who had wanted to marry her but whom she rejected; John Maynard Keynes, the economist; Roger Fry, the painter whose biography Virginia later wrote; and T. S. Eliot, the poet whose lines like "In the room the women come and go, talking of Michelangelo" often sang in my head.

"I understand," she said, "that you have been traveling. Where have you been?"

"Germany, Poland, Russia, and the Soviet Arctic."

"The Soviet Arctic!" Leonard called out.

I turned to look at him.

"I didn't think," he said, hunching closer, "that the Russians allowed anyone to go up there."

"They said I was the first journalist."

"And you were writing for whom?" he asked.

"The *New York Herald Tribune*."

"How old are you?"

"Twenty-four."

"And how old were you when you wrote your essay on Virginia?"

"Twenty."

Virginia seemed not to be listening, drifting off, when her housekeeper Lotte entered with a tray of teacups. She handed me one, but I put it on a small table next to me. I was afraid my hands would tremble and I would drop the cup. Virginia sipped her tea gracefully and began to speak again.

"We were just in your Germany," she said.

Why did she call it *my* Germany? True, the thesis had been published as a trade paperback by the Tauchnitz Press in Leipzig. The publishing house, then 100 years old, was famous for printing the books of English and American authors such as Jane Austen, Charles Dickens, Mark Twain, and Virginia Woolf, all for tourists who could not read German and wanted to read a good book while traveling. To be sure, I had sent her my first letter in 1931 while I was a student at Cologne University. But I had sent the published book from my home in Brooklyn in 1935. She had sent her answer to me in Brooklyn, and I had spoken with a New York accent.

"We were driving through Bonn, on holiday," she said. "Our car was stopped to let Hitler and his entourage pass."

From her diary of April 2, 1935, I later read her impressions as she watched the Nazi convoy:

> *Hitler, very impressive, very frightening. . . . No ideals except equality, superiority, force, possessions.*

*And the passive heavy slaves behind him, and he a
great mould coming down the brown jelly.**

In her parlor, puffing her cigarette, Virginia Woolf shook her
head, still talking of Germany.

"Madness, that country. Madness."

I felt I could talk comfortably about Germany; I had lived
there from 1931 to 1932.

"When I was an exchange student in Cologne," I said, aware
that Leonard was moving his chair closer to me, "I went to a Hitler
rally held in a *Messehalle*, a huge hall near the Rhine. The family
I lived with was terrified that I might be arrested, but I was determined to find out what that madman was really like.

"There were guards and soldiers everywhere, but no one
stopped me and I entered the hall with trepidation. I found a seat
in a half-filled balcony near the stage. A brass band struck up
marching music as, within minutes, the hall filled up with an army
of stormtroopers in brown uniforms and heavy black boots, marching and waving flags with swastikas."

I paused. Had I talked too much?

Leonard moved his chair closer, as Virginia took the cigarette
holder out of her mouth. I went on:

"The crowd went wild when Hitler entered and goose-
stepped to the podium, followed by his entourage. The audience
shouted, screamed, some applauded, others wiped their eyes in
rapture. My heart was beating so loud, I thought one of those SS
men would surely hear and maybe throw me out. But no one
approached me.

"The moment Hitler raised his right hand in salute, the band
stopped playing, the stormtroopers stopped marching, the flags
stopped waving. Hitler's worshippers stood frozen."

Leonard nodded, as if to encourage me to go on. Virginia had
still not resumed smoking.

"Hitler," I said, "was ranting against the Weimar Republic,
ranting against America, and mostly against Jews. It was a hysteri-

*It was probably not Hitler, as Virginia had thought, but, according to most
scholars, Hermann Goering, the head of the German Air Force and one of
Hitler's closest allies.

cal voice that seemed to come not from his throat, but from his bowels. Terrifying."

"He *has* a terrifying voice," Virginia agreed. "There is such horror in the world."

I took up courage to say more.

"Hitler's stormtroopers are now burning books in the university courtyard."

I wondered if they were burning a copy of the paperback book I had sent her.

"What strikes me so forcefully in your books," I said, "is the hope that women will help end the horror and create peace. Men make wars, not women."

"Once," she said, "we had such hope for the world."

The words rang in my head. *Such hope for the world.*

I stood up. Half an hour had passed. I knew I should not take more of her time. I bent over and shook her hand.

"Thank you so much. Your writing gives me the will to write as a woman."

She nodded, "Thank you."

Leonard took my arm and led me out into Tavistock Square.

I returned to my hotel and swiftly jotted notes in my notebook, though I needed no notes to remember this day. I would remember it all vividly for the rest of my life. I was in rapture. I had met Virginia Woolf.

It was late October 1935 when I left London and sailed home on the SS *Normandie.* In the busy New York harbor, I looked around the pier. No one was there to meet me. I guessed my family was getting used to my comings and goings. I tossed my suitcase into the trunk of a yellow cab, and in the taxi's back seat clutched my camera bag and checked my briefcase to make sure that my notebooks and the Virginia Woolf book were all safe.

Driving through Manhattan, then across the Williamsburg Bridge to Brooklyn, I kept breathing the air. Free air. Everything seemed peaceful, serene. The crowded streets seemed purely American with pushcart sellers selling fresh vegetables, while other vendors shouted, "Bargains, everybody. Come get your bargains here," as they pointed to the housedresses hanging from racks. The dark shadow of war had not yet crossed the Atlantic.

I had scarcely rung the doorbell on Harmon Street when Mama opened the heavy black gate, kissed me, and said, "You must be starving."

"Not at all."

"Come in the kitchen anyway." Mama, in a starched white apron, hurried me inside. "I prepared a whole meal for you."

To Mama, food was love. I knew I was home.

In the sun-filled kitchen–dining–living room, Papa sat at the head of the table, waiting for me. I kissed him as he put his arm around me. "Thank the Almighty you're safe," he murmured. I took my favorite seat at his right. Mama was already filling our soup bowls with hot chicken noodle soup; and then she sat down to join us.

"We were so worried about you," Mama said, "when we got your letters from Germany, Poland, Russia. All you hear on the radio is Hitler with that little mustache. He looks like Charlie Chaplin. Who goes to those countries now? Nobody. Only my *mishuggeneh* [crazy] daughter."

She looked at Papa to make sure he agreed. He said nothing but smiled at me. Mama went on, "My aunt Mirel in Poland wrote us you left a lot of your clothes with her granddaughter Hannah."

"I wish I could have brought her to America. She's fifteen. In a couple of years, they'll marry her off. What future does she have?" I turned to Papa. "What future did you have in Odessa?"

Papa stroked his white mustache for a minute. "I had to leave Odessa," he said, "when I was sixteen. That's when the police picked you up, put you in the army, and nobody ever saw you again."

I decided it was safe to tell them something I had never written about to them, knowing how worried they would be. "In your *shtetl*, Mama, I was sitting with all your relatives who wanted to know about everyone in America until two o'clock in the morning. Suddenly two Polish policemen came banging on the door. One of them, a fat one, said, 'We hear you have somebody from America.' He pointed a club at me. 'Open your bags.' I opened my suitcase and watched him silently holding everything, even my panties and bra, up to the candle light. Then he went into my briefcase, opened every book, even a copy of my Virginia Woolf book, and shook them all."

"Those police can't read, can they?" Mama looked defiant.

"Certainly not English. I was worried they might take my notebooks with all my notes. But they left the notebooks alone. I must have looked very suspicious to them, especially carrying a typewriter and a camera. They told me to get out of Poland by morning or I'd be arrested."

"What I was always afraid of," Mama sighed.

"Your Aunt Mirel looked shaken. 'You must go right now,' she said. 'You don't know what they can do to you, arrest you, maybe, God forbid, kill you.' Mirel's son Yankel put me in his wagon, covered me with straw up to my neck, and made his poor old horse go faster and faster until we got to Warsaw."

Papa put his head in his hands. "That was Poland? What happened to you in Germany? We read every day that hundreds of Jewish men are thrown in concentration camp. Jews can't work. Even Jewish judges can't sit in court any more. Jewish children can't go to school. You weren't scared?"

"It was scary sometimes," I admitted. "Hitler has been in power almost three years and the country is completely changed. Completely Nazified. But there were some very brave people, real fighters. I went to see a woman in Berlin, a Jewish social worker. She kept looking out the window, to make sure the SS didn't see me enter her office. 'My daughter is your age,' she told me. 'She can't get out. No visa. No country wants us. Go home and scream. Go home and scream in America what Hitler is doing to us.'"

The kitchen–dining room fell silent. A thought flashed across my mind. We're three thousand miles away from Virginia Woolf. Except for mentioning my book about her, we haven't said one word about her. We were fixated on the terrible news from Germany.

"What did Hitler do to your friends?" Mama persisted.

"I found a few of them. They all had to leave the university. One told me his Ph.D. thesis was stolen from his locker. It was his only copy. He's desperate to get out of Germany. But the lines are so long with people trying to get out."

"Master of the Universe," Mama said, looking up to the heavens. "He took care of you."

I didn't sleep well that night. Images of Virginia Woolf in front of her fireplace, Leonard hunching over to hear about the Soviet Arctic, the talk about Hitler's terrifying voice all kaleidoscoped in my head. Long past midnight, I finally fell asleep.

The next day, I called on Helen Rogers Reid, the wife of the *New York Herald Tribune*'s publisher Ogden Reid, and George Cornish, the senior editor. They were not interested in my interview with Virginia Woolf. "Ruth," Helen Reid said, "we want to hear about your trip to the Soviet Arctic. You know you scooped the world."

George Cornish nodded. "We want you to write a series of four articles on your experiences up there."

The articles were syndicated and then appeared full-page four Sundays in a row, with the photos I had taken. The *Trib* received a score of letters, but none of them meant as much to me as Helen Reid telling me I'd scooped the world.

Virginia Woolf began to recede from my mind when Max Schuster, head of Simon and Schuster, asked me if I had enough unpublished material to write a book on the Soviet Arctic. I could hardly believe my luck when I signed the contract. I realized how timely such a book could be. War was in the air. The Arctic, at the top of the world, would soon serve as the shortest distance between the continents. Planes from New York, Chicago, and California could fly across Alaska to the Soviet Arctic, then across eleven time zones to Moscow, bringing butter and guns. A book I had planned to write on women in a changing world would have to wait until I finished this one.

I Went to the Soviet Arctic was published on September 1, 1939, the very day Hitler's tanks and trucks and armies blasted into Poland. The war in Europe had begun. Virginia Woolf and the book on women were relegated to the drawer in the filing cabinet where the three letters written in 1935 and 1936 would be found almost seventy years later.

My life now revolved around the war and refugees fleeing from Hitler. I was determined to try to help them. But how? I was helpless, frustrated, angry. There were frightening rumors that Hitler was murdering whole villages of Jews in Poland. If only we could rescue them, snatch them from Hitler's clutches. Were our own relatives in danger? What was happening to Hannah? Papa sent money for her older sister to go to *Eretz Israel*—the Land of Israel, the Holy Land. Her parents sat the seven days of mourning for her, weeping. They were sure the Arabs would cut her throat. Later we learned that she was the only one in the family who survived the war.

The United States was still not at war, though most of Europe was burning. Refugees were running across the face of Europe, trying to flee Hitler and his bombs and hordes of soldiers.

Pearl Harbor, December 7, 1941—a date of infamy, our president called it. Now we were fully at war. There were thousands—no, tens of thousands—of Jewish refugees fleeing Hitler's armies. But America's doors were shut. We saved famous people—Albert Einstein, Thomas Mann, Lion Feuchtwanger.* But the so-called "common people," though they were not really common at all, were barred.

Virginia Woolf receded even further into the back of my mind, and, after her suicide in 1941, with no new books or essays appearing, she receded in the minds of others in America, and in England. American and British feminists rediscovered her in the '60s and '70s. Books and articles about her began to appear.

Dr. Deborah F. Stanley, president of SUNY Oswego, told me one evening how Virginia Woolf influenced her life. "She was really seminal in my awakening to the importance of feminism. It was in the seventies. I was at Syracuse University and formed a women's reading group. We were four young women who sat around evenings discussing Virginia Woolf and exploring our souls."

I learned what I had not known while writing my dissertation: she suffered severely from manic depression (the disease is now called "bipolar disorder" by scientists and psychiatrists). One of its manifestations is the tendency to suicide. In 1940, as Nazi planes were bombing Britain, she asked Leonard to buy poison for both of them. She knew that if the Nazis invaded England, Leonard, as a Jew, could be arrested and even murdered. London was on fire.

Virginia, tired, ill, seeking shelter from the nightly incendiary bombs, was ready to give up. She confided cryptically in her diary on May 15, 1940, "If England defeated: What point in waiting? Better shut the garage doors."

Nor had I known that twice, in deep depression, she had tried

---

*Lion Feuchtwanger was a German Jewish novelist, whose book *The Oppermanns*, for which I wrote a preface in 2001, was called "extraordinary" by the *New York Times*. "No single historical or fictional work has more tellingly or insightfully depicted. . . the insidious manner in which Nazism began to permeate the fabric of German society than Lion Feuchtwanger's great novel."

to commit suicide. When she was very young, she kept hearing birds singing in her head in Greek. In 1941, at 59, she put stones in her pockets and walked into the river Ouse.

The time I had spent with her and Leonard was apparently one of her better days. She seemed neither manic nor depressed, but vitally alive. By a strange coincidence, not knowing that Virginia suffered from bipolar disorder, I had written repeatedly in my thesis about the polarity of her writing.

"A law of polarity, of conflicts as irreconcilable, as endless as night and day, reverberates through all of Virginia Woolf's writing and reaches ultimate expression in *The Waves*," as I wrote in my essay.

Even in her struggle for a style, she describes swinging from doubt in herself to "an ebb and flow of self-confidence, of doubt, of attempted change, and grim resolution."

The odyssey of how I met Virginia Woolf, and how her life and work became intertwined with my life as an exchange student in Germany, began, oddly enough, when, in the autumn of 1926, at fifteen, I entered New York University and took my first course in German. Already a lover of Beethoven and Bach, I spent my undergraduate years learning more about the land and the culture that had produced them, and the language they spoke.

Ending my sophomore year, I spent the summer vacation in a six-week German program at Mount Holyoke College. The program was filled with American professors of German who came as students and who, despite my denials, were convinced that I was the granddaughter of Franz Gruber, the author of "Silent Night, Holy Night."

English was *verboten*—prohibited. We ate, studied, sang, talked, and, I swear, even dreamed in German. Often, after morning classes and a hot New England lunch, I climbed a hill and shouted German poetry into the winds. German became my second language, and it was to be my mainstay when I brought a thousand refugees to America in 1944. German was the lingua franca of central Europe.

After spending another summer at Harvard, this time studying Shakespeare, I had enough credits to graduate from NYU, in three years, My philology professor, Dr. Ernst Prokosch, suggested that I apply for a fellowship to the German

Department at the University of Wisconsin. Prokosch's name on a letter of recommendation was magic. Within weeks, a letter arrived from Wisconsin:

"We congratulate you on being selected for the LaFrentz Fellowship in the graduate program of the German Department. You will receive full tuition and a stipend of $600."

I was elated. Fellowships were one of the ways students survived during the Depression. In August 1929, I left for Madison, Wisconsin, planning to hitchhike the whole way. Instead of trying to stop me, Papa was so proud that he took me to his service station to get maps of the best route. No one worried. The roads were full of students holding up signs such as "CHICAGO HERE I COME" or "LA OR BUST." Hitchhiking in those days was safe and fun. Truck drivers, often lonely on long drives, were glad to have someone to talk to. My one mistake was landing in a whorehouse in Troy, New York. One of the girls, in a tight-fitting blue satin dress and high-heeled blue satin shoes, stared at me in my brown oxfords and white socks, my blue skirt and white blouse. I looked more like a fifteen-year-old than eighteen in that outfit.

"Hey, kid," she said, "what are you doing here?"

"I'm on my way to college in Wisconsin."

"Well, you better get out of here fast. This is no place for you."

That one year from 1930 to '31 in Wisconsin was a year of stretching, of walking along the shores of the beautiful lakes, trying to discover who I was, making new friends, and writing my masters' thesis in the German Department on Goethe's *Faust*.

While in Wisconsin, I applied for a second grant, this time to travel to Germany, given by the Institute of International Education, known by the letters IIE.

The letter telling me I had won the fellowship and could study in Germany from 1931 to 1932 arrived during Easter vacation. I decided the news was too good to tell my parents by phone, so I hitchhiked home. Impatient after a full day, I decided to take a train from Albany to Manhattan's Penn Station. I telephoned our housekeeper, telling her to ask my parents to meet me.

I learned later that in the Studebaker, driving from our house in Brooklyn to Manhattan, Mama asked suspiciously, "Dave, why is she coming home now? She didn't even come home for Christmas. I tell you, she must be pregnant."

Papa, who never lost faith in me, tried to reassure her. "Wait. We'll find out soon enough."

At the station, I flung my arms around them. "Guess what," I could hardly control my excitement, "I'm going to Germany!"

Mama shook her head. "I wish she was pregnant."

Unlike their pride in the Wisconsin fellowship, this exchange fellowship to Germany was a nightmare for them. They did their best to prevent me from going. They offered me a car. They offered me the equivalent in money. Mama was sure that Adolf Hitler, who was not yet in power in 1931 but was in the news almost every day, would come off a stage and shoot me.

"He won't shoot me, Mom," I told her. "I'll wear a pin with an American flag on my lapel and I'll carry my American passport in my blouse."

Mama, sharp-eyed and sharp-tongued, said, "And Hitler can't shoot through a passport?"

I told my father, "Papa, you knew at sixteen it was time for you to leave Odessa. You knew you had to get out of Czarist Russia. I know it's time for me to go to Germany. I want to find out what Hitler is up to."

Though I knew how anxious they were, I had the money in my pocket. Restless to get out of Brooklyn and begin my journey, I gave myself the whole summer to travel through Europe. The classes in Cologne would start in late September.

Seeing me off on the S.S. *Milwaukee* of the Hamburg-Amerika Line, Mama wept. "I don't know if we'll ever see you again."

"You will, Mama. It's only for one year."

She acted as if she were already sitting in mourning.

It was June 1931 when I arrived in Paris and spent a month taking morning classes at the Sorbonne and whiling away my afternoons sipping tea at the Metropol Café, hoping to see some of the American writers in exile, especially Ernest Hemingway and Gertrude Stein. I never saw them, but I was thrilled, telling myself the world was opening up for me.

London was next. I took my first airplane ride from Paris to London. I felt like an adventurer. I was exploring two cities I had grown to love from books. I was also exploring myself, a nineteen-year-old who had grown up in the cocoon of a loving Jewish family, yearning to break free, yearning to embrace the world. I was happy to travel alone so that no one diverted me from meeting new people and marveling at the beauty of these two cities. Elsewhere in England, I wandered through Oxford, visited Stratford where Shakespeare had lived, and breathed the literary air of England so that Charles Dickens's novels and Wordsworth's poetry came alive to me as never before.

From London I took a train and ferry to Holland, sat on its beautiful beach at Scheveningen, watched Dutch women walk in wooden clogs, and finally arrived in Cologne on a balmy September day in 1931.

Dr. Hugo Gabriel, thirtyish and effervescent, representing the IIE at the University, had found a Jewish home for me with Papa Otto and Mama Frieda Herz and their daughter Luisa, my age. They treated me as if I were their second daughter.

For some reason, as soon as we met, Dr. Gabriel told me that his parents were Jewish, but he was Protestant. Hitler was not yet in power, but some Jews, fearing his virulent anti-Semitic threats, sought to save themselves by converting. I did not feel that I had the right to ask him why he had abandoned his Jewishness.

He helped me choose the courses I would take. We agreed that I would attend classes in German Philosophy with the renowned Nietzsche scholar Ernst Bertram; "Englisches Seminar"; and art history.

I had been at the university for about a month when Professor Herbert Schöffler, a round, fatherly-looking, middle-aged man, head of the "Englisches Seminar," called me to his office.

"We have been watching you," he said. "We would like you to stay and work for a Ph.D."

A Ph.D.!

I shook my head. "My parents would never give me money to stay for another two or three years—or however long it takes to get a Ph.D. in Germany."

"Nobody," Professor Schöffler was smiling, "nobody in Germany has ever gotten a doctorate in one year. But maybe you can do it. I have a special reason. I love Virginia Woolf's writing. None of my students knows English well enough to analyze her writing. You are the only American student here. I would like you to write a dissertation—in English—analyzing her work, her style, her language."

I managed to say "I'll try," shook his hand, and rushed downtown to my favorite bookstore. There they were, all of her novels published to that point, including her latest, *The Waves*, all in English, all in paperback, all published by the Tauchnitz Press.

I was soon mesmerized by Virginia Woolf's writing. I hung her picture on my bedroom wall. *A Room of One's Own* became my Bible. It gave me the courage to later dispense with the objective journalist's voice and write from my heart and soul. I was fascinated by her will to write as a woman, and distraught by her anxiety and fear that male critics would tear her books apart. She was on the side of the creators, the dreamers, the poets, the women. On the other side were the critics, the predators, the destroyers, the angry, hostile, women-loathing men.

She wrote *Orlando*, my favorite of her novels, as an ode to Vita Sackville-West, one of the women she loved. In a sense, the character "Orlando" was physically bipolar—a charming and heroic man who metamorphoses into a charming and beautiful woman.

In one of my sessions with Professor Schöffler, I told him how much I was enjoying Woolf's writing and how much more I wanted to know about her.

"Very good," he said. "Why don't you write to her, care of the Hogarth Press?"

He checked his files and gave me the address, "52 Tavistock Square, London, W.C.1, and here is her telephone number, Museum 3488."

I wrote a letter which included some questions about her work and, a few weeks later, received an answer from her secretary, Peggy Bolsher.

16th Dec 1931

Dear Madam,

> *. . . Mrs Woolf has always preferred to let her readers decide for themselves as to the meaning of her books, and therefore can not reply to your questions as to the autobiographical elemkent [sic] in Orlando; but it is generally known that the story is based, so far as it is*

based on reality, on the life of Miss Sackville West; and the house is underatood [sic] to be Knole, the home of Miss Wests [sic] ancestors in Kent.

Yours faithfully
P. Bolsher
(Secretary)

During the Christmas vacation, I took some of Virginia Woolf's books with me on the train to Berchtesgaden, Hitler's favorite vacation town. I was with four other American exchange students, each of us invited by the U.S. State Department to spend the holiday together at a ski lodge. A State Department official greeted us as we entered the lodge, told us he was in charge and that if we had any problems, we were to come to him.

He told us to meet for dinner at 6 P.M. in the ski lodge. Five townspeople were our hosts, all jovial-looking, the women in brightly colored dirndl skirts and starched white blouses, the men in knee-high leather pants, leather vests, plaid shirts, and green felt hats with feathers darting up from the brim. I was placed next to a robust, red-faced peasant in his mid-twenties. After he had drunk several beers, he became a little too friendly, putting his arm around my waist.

"You're different, even though you're an American," he said to me in German. "I don't like Americans, and I hate Jews."

I pulled his arm away, stood up, and said, "I am an American, I am a Jew, and I will not listen to anyone denouncing my country and my people." I stalked out.

The State Department official rushed after me. "You insulted him. I want you to go back and apologize."

"I apologize to someone who denounces America and Jews? *He* should apologize to *me*."

The State Department official's face flushed with anger. "This is no way to treat our host."

"Then I will leave here in the morning."

Back in my bedroom, freezing with cold, I asked for hot bricks for my feet. They were poor comfort for the anger I felt that a U.S. governmental official would defend an obvious Nazi. True, I was his guest, but I did not have to submit to a Nazi insult. I was angry too that the official was more concerned with proper manners than with racial slurs.

I packed my clothes and my Virginia Woolf books the next morning and took a train to Vienna, where a friend of my sister Betty was studying medicine.

"What would you like to see today?" he asked me.

"I'd like to the see the university where you're studying."

"I don't think you're going to like what I have to show you."

"Why?"

"You'll see."

We entered the lab; broken glass lay strewn on long tables and on the floor.

"Nazis came in here yesterday," he told me, "and broke every one of our experiments. Months of work ruined."

"It's horrible," I said. "How can you go on studying here?"

"I have no choice. I couldn't get into a medical school in the States. They all have quotas limiting the number of Jewish students. I was lucky to be accepted here, and I'm going to stay."

I left Vienna, rushed back to Cologne, and continued working on the dissertation while attending courses on Nietszche, modern English literature, and Albrecht Dürer in art history. At the same time, I followed the results of the German elections that were taking place every few months. The greatest lesson I learned in Germany was how one can become a dictator *legally*. Hitler entered every election and won nearly all of them until he reached the top and overthrew the government.

In the summer of 1932, I handed Professor Schöffler my thesis, "Virginia Woolf: A Study." A few days later, I would take the oral examinations. Three examiners—Professor Bertram, Professor Schöffler, and a professor from the art department—sat on chairs in a circle in Bertram's office, like inquisitors in an interrogation chamber. One of my Jewish friends in the university had told me that Professor Bertram hated Jews. hated Americans, and hated women. But he was a charismatic teacher who had taught us enthusiastically about what a great philosopher Nietzsche was.

Stories of how many students Professor Bertram had failed in their orals flashed through my brain. German students could take them over and over, but if I failed, it was the end for me.

I stood before the three men, my hands cold as ice. Professor

16

Bertram, speaking in German, began the ordeal with questions about Nietzsche and his philosophy.

"What stands out most for you in Nietzsche's philosophy?" he asked.

I tried to control my teeth from chattering,

"His search to lead the German people to new heights, to help Germany rise above even the evils we see confronting her today."

What if he's a Nazi? I thought. How will he react to my talking about evil today?

But he went on, asking more questions, until I startled myself by shouting my favorite Nietzsche line, "*Nacht bin ich, ach dass ich Licht ware* [Night am I; ah, that I were light]."

Professor Schöffler took over. Beads of sweat ran into my eyes.

"In your thesis," Professor Schöffler began, "you describe how much more sympathetic Virginia Woolf's women are than most of her men. Please explain this."

"For Virginia Woolf," I said, "woman is the creator, man is the destroyer. Many of her women are heroic, her men often weak, with no heart, no mind."

Now why did I say that, I wondered. I saw Bertram and the art professor sitting straight, listening hard, their faces frozen.

"You call her novel *The Waves* a 'rhythm of conflicts,'" Professor Schoffler said. "What did you mean?"

I managed to pull out of my brain sentences still fresh from my thesis. "It's the struggle between light and darkness. It is the law of polarity, of conflicts as irreconcilable as night and day, of poets versus critics, that reverberates through all her writing."

The third inquisitor, the art professor, interrogated me about Albrecht Dürer.

The inquisition lasted half an hour. The three men rose, and Professor Schöffler led me to the door, telling me to wait outside.

A few minutes later, he came toward me. "I am proud to tell you, Fräulein Gruber, you have won your doctorate *mit sehr gut*. It's the German equivalent of your American 'magna cum laude.'"

I was speechless.

Professor Bertram came out to shake my hand. "*Schicken Sie uns recht viel Jugend genäu wie Sie.*" ("Send us many more young people just like you.")

I was still dazed when Professor Schöffler handed me two sheets of paper. "These are Professor Bertram's and my critiques of your dissertation on Virginia Woolf."

I read Schöffler's first: "It is a critical study of a woman by a woman. A man could never have written this work. It possesses deep critical powers and a profound knowledge of English and world literature."

Still disbelieving, I read Bertram's page: "This work could be a model for modern criticism. The struggle of the poet with the critic is seen very sharply, very clearly. The work shows amazing maturity and originality."

I ran all the way home to share the news with my German family.

"*Fräulein Doktor*," Mama Herz embraced me.

The next day, I traveled to Frankfurt, determined to see Goethe's house before I left Germany. I stood in awe at the desk where Germany's greatest poet, playwright, and novelist had written his masterpieces, some with a quill pen. In the ladies' room, I listened in shock as an attendant with a bosom projecting like a bulwark screamed at a small elderly woman. "You pig. You asshole. You dog manure. I clean these stinking toilets and you give me one pfennig."

"But that's all the money I have." The lady hunched her body protectively.

"You're a stinking liar. Get out now before I tear you apart."

I helped the old woman out, and gave a handful of coins to the attendant, who was stamping on a rumpled newspaper. As she moved away, something drew me to look down. I saw my face printed in the newspaper. This foul-mouthed ogre had been wiping her feet on my picture!

The caption read,

20 JAHRE ALT—UND SCHON "FRL. DR."
IN EINEM JAHR GESCHAFT

[20 years old and already Fräulein Doktor.
Achieved in one year]

The article told the story:

> *At 20, she is the youngest Ph.D. in the University of Cologne and the youngest Ph.D. in Germany. An exchange student, she came for one year to study in Germanistik and Anglistik and Art History. When her great talents were recognized, it was suggested to her that she try to work on her doctorate. After one year, she had the Doctor Diploma in her pocket. Our young doctor, despite all her knowledge, has still remained very young, and is overjoyed to be in Germany.*

I took the train back to Cologne, where Mama Herz greeted me excitedly: "*Kindchen* (Child), the office of the *Oberburgermeister* [the Lord Mayor] Doctor Konrad Adenauer telephoned you to come to the *Rathaus* (city hall) tomorrow morning at nine o'clock."

Why would Dr. Adenauer want to see me? He was the beloved mayor who had been returned to office in every election since 1917.*

Long before nine, I was in front of the *Rathaus*. It was a massive stone building, with Romanesque arches, built in 1150 in the Jewish quarter of Cologne. The street sign said: *Judengasse*, the Street of the Jews.

Nazi hecklers in the university, strutting in their brown uniforms, black boots, and swastikas on their arms, often shouted at me, "We should drive the Jews out. They don't belong here," as if Jews were newcomers. The Rathaus and the street sign were evidence that Jews had been living in Germany for more than eight hundred years.

Dr. Adenauer's office, on the Street of the Jews, was a huge chamber with heavy drapes and thick carpets, flooded with sunlight. Dr. Adenauer, tall and stately, with high cheekbones, a prominent nose, and skin the color of ivory, towered over me as he shook my hand.

"I congratulate you. You have done what no German student has done."

I murmured, "Thank you."

"I have a present for you from the people of Cologne."

---

*After World War II, he became even more famous for facing up to the evil the Nazis had wrought and worked on compensating victims of the Holocaust.

He presented me with two beautifully illustrated art books of his city.

He opened one to show me photos and paintings that told the story of Cologne.

"We hope you will come back to Cologne, Fräulein Doktor," Mayor Adenauer said. "Until you do, I trust these books will help you remember your year among us."

"I promise you, I will never forget this year, nor will I forget you."

He placed his hand on my head as in a benediction. "Bless you, my child. May God go with you."

A few days after my meeting with Mayor Adenauer, I took the train to Hamburg, and there climbed aboard the *St. Louis*, the flagship of the Hamburg-Amerika Line.*

Sailing home in 1932, I spent most of my time on deck, rereading passages from some of my favorite Virginia Woolf novels. Coming down the gangway in New York, I saw a crowd of reporters and photographers on the pier. The men had press cards standing up in the ribbons of their felt hats. I looked back up the gangway to see if some movie star was coming down; a rumor had spread during the crossing that Mary Pickford was traveling in first class.

Suddenly, the army of reporters surrounded me. One of them shouted, "How does it feel to be the youngest Ph.D. in the world?" Another called out, "Read yesterday's *New York Times*. They say you're the youngest in the whole world. How do you feel about that?"

How could I answer these reporters? I had never been interviewed before. After Germany, the crush of men around me seemed like an invasion. I had to escape. I pushed through the crowd and found Mama and Papa and my brother Irving.

"Get me out of here," I panted.

We drove swiftly. In the car, Mama told me how the phone hadn't stopped ringing. "Reporters were asking, 'When is your daughter coming back?' Our neighbors, especially the German ones, are

---

*This was the same ship that would carry 1,000 Jewish refugees from Germany in 1939. All of them had legal visas to Cuba; but when they reached the Caribbean, they were denied entrance by Cuban officials. Their brave captain then took the ship of desperate refugees to Florida. But they were not allowed to land there either. They had no visas to enter America. They were forced to sail back to Europe, where most of them were later trapped, sent to concentration camps, and killed.

sending so many flowers, the house looks like the Botanical Garden."

Papa, driving the car, turned for a moment to look at me. "I guess we were wrong trying to stop you from going."

At home I ran up to my bedroom and threw myself onto the bed, weeping. I didn't know why I was crying. I think I cried because the girl I had been was no more, and now I was safe in America, while a dark cloud hung over the Herzes and all the Jews of Germany.

The phone rang for three days, and Mama bravely lied to the reporters: "She's out of town."

But one day, she came up to my room and said, "There's a reporter sitting on our doorsteps. He's from the *New York Herald Tribune*. He says he'll sit there all night if you don't talk to him. He says he'll lose his job if he doesn't get the story."

"I can't do it, Mom."

"It's not right," Mama said. "You can't let the poor man sit on our stoop all night. Go outside. He won't chop your head off."

I washed my face and went out to the stoop, walked down the stairs, and sat next to a middle-aged man with a battered face and a battered hat.

"I appreciate your seeing me," he said gently. "I guess you're overwhelmed. I would be too."

His article appeared on Sunday, September 4, 1932, headlined:

**GIRL PH.D., 20, BEWILDERED BY
FUSS OVER FEAT**

**RUTH GRUBER FEELS HUNTED,
SHE SAYS: FEELS ACHIEVEMENT
WAS NOT UNUSUAL**

HAD FUN WHILE STUDYING

**JUST WANTS SOLITUDE A WHILE
TO GET HER BEARINGS**

More reporters demanded interviews; more articles appeared. The most amusing one was in the *New York Evening Post*, titled: "Sex and Intellect," pointing out that a young woman had done what no young man had done, gotten a Ph.D. at 20.

Despite the publicity, I could not get a job. The Depression was on, and if there were jobs, they went to young men, not young women. I tried freelancing and, after a stack of rejections, sold an article to the Sunday *New York Times*. It was on Brooklyn, which I called a microcosm of Europe. The *Herald Tribune* then bought several more articles, which I enjoyed writing. I had never taken a course in journalism, but I learned on the job and began to feel that maybe I was making my way in the world.

At the same time, I found another part-time job. At Romany Marie's restaurant in Greenwich Village, I met the American explorer of the Arctic, Vilhjalmur Stefansson, who hired me to translate into English the German documents he needed for a massive study of the Arctic countries of the world that he was writing for the War Department.

My dream was to leave Brooklyn and live in Greenwich Village, but none of my jobs paid enough to let me leave home. I applied to the Guggenheim Foundation and, with their recommendation, won a grant to go abroad given by the New Jersey Federation of Women's Clubs. It was 1935, and it was my third fellowship. My project was to write a book on women under fascism, communism, and democracy. It occurred to me that while in London, I might be able to interview Virginia Woolf for my study of women.

When I told George Cornish, the editor at the *Herald Tribune*, that I was going abroad, he said, "You can be our special foreign correspondent and send us articles that you think will interest us."

I was still home when a letter came from Professor Schöffler telling me that the Tauchnitz Press, of which he was literary editor, had decided to publish my doctoral thesis on Virginia Woolf in a trade paperback edition. It was three years since I had written the dissertation, but now it was coming out in Germany from the same publisher that had published all of Virginia Woolf's books. "You're in good company," Professor Schöffler wrote.*

---

*Only later did I learn that Professor Schöffler was Jewish, and that he had fallen victim to the Nazis. When the SS knocked on his door, he killed himself. Dr. Hugo Gabriel, the Protestant convert from Judaism who had been my adviser at the University of Cologne, and whom I later helped get a visa to come to New York in the late 1930s, told me of Professor Schöffler's death. Tears formed behind my eyes. I owed him so much. Why couldn't I have helped him get a visa?

Excitedly, I worked on the galleys of the book, corrected some minor printer's errors, and finally held it in my hands. It was my first published book, bound in the same light green cover in which the Tauchnitz Press had published Virginia's works. It would be sent, the publishers told me, to universities in America, Germany, and England. I found it on sale in Barnes and Noble, which was then housed in one small bookshop in lower Manhattan. It sold for $1.50, a good price in 1935. Hardcovers sold for $2.95 or $3.95.

With apprehension and the chutzpah of youth, I sent the book to Virginia Woolf, with this letter:

14 Harmon Street
Brooklyn, New York

May 8, 1935

Mrs. Virginia Woolf
The Hogarth Press
52, Tavistock Square
London, W.C.1

Dear Mrs. Woolf,

I am sending you a copy of a book I have written about your work. Although dated 1934, the publication was unfortunately delayed and the book has just appeared.

I wrote the book while living in Germany, where, as you no doubt know, you are regarded, and I feel it is with justice, as England's foremost novelist.

I shall be deeply interested in your opinion of the book.

Sincerely yours,
Ruth Gruber

On May 17, 1935, the manager of the Hogarth Press, Margaret West, answered my letter.

The Hogarth Press
52 Tavistock Square,
London, W.C. 1

May 17th, 1935.

Miss Ruth Gruber,
14 Harmon Street,
Brooklyn,
New York,
U.S.A.

Dear Madam,
Your letter of May 8th and the book to which you refer, addressed to Mrs. Virginia Woolf, have been received during her absence in Italy. They will be placed before her on her return.
Yours faithfully,
THE HOGARTH PRESS.
Margaret West
MANAGER.

As soon as I received Miss West's letter, I replied,

May 28, 1935

Dear Miss West,
Thank you for your letter of May 17th. I am planning to sail for Europe on the 22nd of June to gather more material for a book I am now working on. I shall probably arrive in England on the 27th of June and should like very much to arrange an interview with Mrs. Woolf if she plans to be in or near London at that time. May I expect to hear from you soon?
Sincerely yours,
Ruth Gruber

I had real doubts that Virginia Woolf would agree to invite me. But I figured she would either allow me to interview her, or instruct her secretary to tell me she was too busy.

She did, of course, invite me, but I knew nothing about her physical or mental health when I met her. Nor did I know that she kept a diary, the entries of which she usually wrote in the afternoon between tea and dinner. Half a century later, in 1989, I discovered that those diaries—and boxes of her letters—were in the New York Public Library on 5th Avenue at 42nd Street.

To read them, I climbed a flight of stairs, walked down a long hall, and entered a room marked "Berg Collection." It was an elegant oak-paneled reading room that had the air of a cloistered sanctuary. Formal oil paintings of Dr. Henry W. Berg and Dr. Albert A. Berg, separated by a wooden arch with corinthian columns, filled the east wall. A terra cotta figure of Moses, holding the Ten Commandments, stood above the front door.

The Berg brothers were lovers of books and learning. They spent their days working as surgeons at Mt. Sinai Hospital in New York. Then, with a fortune amassed in real estate, they distributed money generously to hospitals and universities and purchased rare manuscripts, which they donated to the room named after them in the library. It was their funds that were used to purchase Virginia Woolf's diaries and letters.

When I convinced the curator, a large, scholarly, and formidable woman, Lola L. Szladits, that I was a serious student of Virginia Woolf's writings, she allowed me to hold some of Woolf's letters in my hands. I was holding the thin blue paper on which she wrote, and I actually felt her presence around me. Her writing was small and crowded, and seemed to have been written in haste.

I was astonished to find myself mentioned in both the diary and the letters in the Berg Collection. Now, with the additional help of the three letters she sent me, I am able to put together a chronology of our correspondence and the relationship between a mature and supremely skillful writer and a young woman struggling to define herself.

Four months before we met, she confided to her diary:

31 May, 1935

> *. . . the usual tremor & restlessness after coming back, and nothing to settle to, & some good German woman sends me a pamphlet on me into which I couldn't resist looking, though nothing so upsets and demor-*

alizes as this looking at one's face in the glass. And a German glass produces an extreme diffuseness and complexity so that I can't get either praise or blame but must begin twisting among long words.

I was amused to find that she called me "some good German woman." I have not an ounce of German blood, and I was born in Brooklyn, New York. I knew, though, what she meant about German writing and how complex German words could be. True, the book was published by the Tauchnitz Press, but I had written my thesis in English, not German, and I had sent the published English book to her from Brooklyn. Just as she could not "get either praise or blame," now I could not tell how she felt about my book. It seemed to me that if she had really read it, instead of saying she "couldn't resist looking," she would have known that I was an ardent admirer of her work.

Three weeks after she wrote this entry in her diary, she sent the first of her three letters to me. These letters—placed chronologically next to her diary and her massive correspondence—helped me to see her in the context of her era in Britain, and to understand the violent swings of her illness and her all-too-real fear that she was going insane.

The first letter, sent from her home in Sussex, was written on June 21, 1935 on fine white linen paper, undamaged by time, with an embossed letterhead.

Monk's House
Rodmell, near
Lewes, Sussex.

Dear Miss Gruber,
I found your book waiting for me on my return from Italy the other day. I think that my secretary explained that I was way [sic] *hence the delay in thanking you. It was very good of you to send me a copy. But I must confess, frankly, that I have not read it, but I am sure you will believe that this is not through laziness or lack of interest in the subject. But the fact is that I try to avoid reading about my own*

writing when I am actually writing.* I find that it makes me self-conscious and for some reason distracts me from my work.

But if I have not read it myself, I have lent it to a friend, who is an excellent critic; and I am told that you have written a most sympathetic and acute study of my books. I wxxx shall read it as soon as I have finished the book I am now working on.

I must thank you sincerely for having taken this interest in my work. That is in itself a great encouragement to me. And I need not say how much I hope that it will have a success with the public.

> *With thanks,*
> *yours sincerely*
> *Virginia Woolf*

Reading it now, from the vantage point of nearly seven decades, I am heartened by her generosity in taking time from her own writing to send it to an "excellent critic" who had called it a "most sympathetic and acute study." Who was the critic? In a corner of my mind, I wondered if the critic was her husband Leonard.

But this newly discovered letter contradicted the notes in her diary that she had written a few weeks earlier, revealing that she *had* looked into the book.

This first letter did not reach me until I returned home to Brooklyn in late October 1935. She had mailed it on June 21, but I had left for Europe on June 22. When the letter arrived in Brooklyn on June 27, 1935, Mama tucked it away in a file drawer for safekeeping.

That very day, I stepped off the SS *Milwaukee* at Southampton and made my way to London. After settling into a hotel, I visited the *Herald Tribune*'s London office, was greeted cordially by the reporters, and then telephoned Jon Kimche, a well-known English journalist whom I had met in New York.

When I told him that I had written a letter to Virginia Woolf and sent her my dissertation in book form, he said, "Why don't you call the Hogarth Press and ask for an interview?"

---

*The book she was writing was *The Years*.

I was less confident than I had been in Brooklyn. "I have a feeling she won't allow me to interview her."

"I'm sure she'd be delighted to meet you. Certainly I would be if somebody wrote a dissertation on my work. Yours is the first English dissertation anyone has written about Virginia Woolf."*

I was still doubtful. "Why would she would want to spend time with me? She must get hundreds of such requests."

"Don't be silly. She can't help but feel flattered. If you're afraid to call, I'll make the call for you."

"Thank you, no. I'll make it myself."

I telephoned the Hogarth Press and reached the manager, Margaret West.

"Mrs. Woolf and her husband," she said, "are on vacation and will be gone for another few weeks. How long will you be in London?"

"A few weeks. Then I will be traveling for four or five months."

"Will you be returning to London?" she asked.

"Yes."

"Do call us as soon as you arrive. We can set up a date for you. Can you tell me now what you plan to interview Mrs. Woolf about?"

"It's for a book I plan to write about women under fascism, communism, and democracy. I would appreciate her views on the role of women in a rapidly changing world."

"Very good," she said. "I will expect to hear from you when you return."

I left London, and for four months traveled across Europe and the Soviet Arctic. On my way back to London, I stopped off in Holland to visit the Herz family, with whom I had lived as an exchange student in Cologne. They had just escaped from Hitler to Amsterdam.[†]

I stayed with Mama and Papa Herz for a few days and, while

---

*At Oxford in 2004, my friend Heidi Stalla, the Junior Dean, who is writing her own Ph.D. thesis on Virginia Woolf, confirmed the reporter's words. "Dozens of other students," she told me, "are writing Ph.D. theses on Virginia Woolf and they all use your book. Yours was the first."

†A Dutch hero later hid the Herz family in a safe house, where they survived. In 1945, my brother Irving, a captain traveling with General Patton's army, found them looking old and skeletal. They flung their arms around him when he told them he was my brother. "Wait here," Irving said, "I'll be right back." He drove to the army PX, filled his truck with provisions, and brought them the first fresh fruits and vegetables they had eaten in two years. Unfortunately, the Dutch hero who had saved them was caught and executed.

there, sent a note to Margaret West at the Hogarth Press, telling her that I would be arriving shortly in London.

Virginia Woolf answered my letter (this is the second letter we found). The envelope showed that she had mailed her answer to me in care of the Herz family in Amsterdam. Papa Herz, in turn, had crossed out their address and forwarded it to 14 Harmon St., Brooklyn. Mama stored it with the first letter in the same safe filing cabinet drawer.

On plain white stationery, the letter read:

52 Tavistock Square London WC 1

12th Oct. 1935

Dear Madam,
I have only just received your letter; and I am afraid that this will not reach you in time.
I should of course be glad to do anything I can to help you in your work; and will arrange to see you if possible. But as I am not a politician and have no special knowledge of the subject on which you are writing I fear that it would probably be only a waste of your time to see me.
If you like to ring up The Hogarth Press Museum 3488 my secretary will take a message. But as I say, I fear that this letter will reach you too late.
Yours sincerely
Virginia Woolf

I think now if I had received this letter in Amsterdam, with its halfhearted invitation addressed to "Dear Madam," I would have hesitated to telephone her. Fortunately, I followed the advice Margaret West had given me. As soon as I reached London, I phoned the Hogarth Press again.

Miss West's answer was gracious: "Mrs. Woolf would like you to come to tea Tuesday, October 15th at 6:00 P.M."

I was ecstatic.

But now, sitting in the Berg Collection, I opened *The Letters of Virginia Woolf Volume Five 1932–1935*. I found my name in the index, and I learned what Virginia Woolf had thought of me before we met on October 15th.

The day before our meeting, she had written to Julian Bell, the nephew she adored, who was teaching English in China and who later died in the Spanish Civil War.

14th Oct 1935

Dearest Julian,
. . . Now I suppose you are teaching the Chinks
('Chinks?')
I must now go and see an importunate and unfortunate Gerwoman who thinks I can help her with facts about Women under Democracy—little she knows—what you do about your poor old Virginia.

Me? Importunate? Unfortunate? Gerwoman? I was shocked by her words. A thin flame of anger was burning my throat.

I was even angrier when I read my name again in the diary, written just before she was coming upstairs to meet me.

Tuesday 15 October

. . . couldn't write this morning; & must go up & receive Miss Grueber [sic] *(to discuss a book on women and fascism—a pure have yer as Lottie would say) in 10 minutes.*

A pure have yer?

"What could it mean?" I asked the curator, Lola L. Szladits.

"No idea what that means," she said, "but maybe the woman sitting over there would know." She pointed to a woman who was studying early drafts of *Mrs. Dalloway.*

I approached Ruth Webb, a friendly school inspector from London. We whispered as if there were other people in the room, though there were none.

"A pure have yer," she repeated, "is cockney. I should know, I come from cockney stock. But really I haven't a clue as to its meaning. All I can tell you is, it's derogatory."

At the information desk I asked Catherine Halls, an English librarian, if she knew what "a pure have yer" meant.

She told me she had never heard the expression.

"It's probably slang. We have a lot of slang dictionaries. They're right over there."

In Eric Partridge's *A Dictionary of Slang and Unconventional English*, I looked up the word: *pure (n.) a mistress, esp. a kept mistress, a wanton, dog's dung.*

My head exploded. *Dog's dung?*

Wait. Perhaps she used *pure* as an adjective and *have* as a noun. In Partridge's *Slang: Today and Yesterday*, I found: *Have (n), a deception, a swindle.*

I felt my blood rising again. Did she think I had come to swindle her? If so, then why had she invited me to tea?

What did she think of me *after* what had been for me a magical half hour in her parlor at 52 Tavistock Square? In her *Letters, Volume Five 1932–1935*, I found an entry about me, and ordered the original letter from the stack. The letter was written to her lover, Ethel Smyth, a seventy-year-old composer, complaining that she had been unable to work. It was six days after my visit.

Monday, 21 October 1935

> *I've had a poetess reading her works aloud [Easdale]; I've had a French socialist declaiming against Fascism [Walter]; I've had a German Jewess [Gruber]— no, I cant go into all the vociferations and gesticulations that are our lot in Tavistock Sqre.*

A German Jewess! Perhaps she decided I was a poor refugee fleeing Hitler, washed up on Britain's shores, importuning her for help.

Years later, anxious to know the truth, I asked Aïda Lovell, one of my friends in London, to write to Nigel Nicolson, the son of Vita Sackville-West, about Virginia Woolf's attitude toward me and about what "a pure have yer" really meant.

Nicolson, who edited many of Woolf's diaries and letters, answered Aïda:

Dr. Gruber won't be too pleased by this, but I was glad to read in VW's diary that she was quite flattered by what Dr. G wrote about her . . . which was rare for Virginia.

I wondered if Nigel Nicolson was confirming what I had read in her first letter to me, in which she wrote that she had lent the book to an "excellent critic," and was told "that you have written a most sympathetic and acute study of my book." The diary entry seemed to confirm that the "critic" was Virginia Woolf herself. Still uncertain, I wrote to Nicolson, who answered,

I fear that you may have been hurt by her references to you, but she was like that in her diaries and letters, though perfectly courteous in conversation. . . . That is one of the things I deplore about Virginia, her cattiness, contempt for almost everyone who were not her friends, an occasional touch of anti-Semitism, her snobbishness and jealousy.

Back in December 1935, still naïve and unaware of her biting comments in her diary and letters, I wrote to her again, taking the liberty of enclosing some material on the Soviet Arctic. Apparently she had written me a letter which I cannot find, but I found the carbon copy on yellow paper of my answer to her:

14 Harmon Street
Brooklyn, New York
December 27, 1935

Mrs. Virginia Woolf
Monk's House
Rodmell, near
Lewes, Sussex

Dear Mrs. Woolf,
I thought this pamphlet showing the Arctic trip we discussed when I saw you last October in London might interest you.

I am wondering whether you have had time yet to read the study I made of your writings. Your reasons for waiting until you had finished your book were splendid, I thought. Now that Christmas has come, and I understood you to say that you would complete the work around Christmas time, I wondered if you had found the opportunity to read the work. I am deeply interested in your opinion of it.

With kindest regards to Mr. Woolf and yourself,
Yours sincerely,
Ruth Gruber

P.S. It may interest you to know that the London News Chronicle *published an article on the Arctic soon after I had spoken of it to you, and that the* Sphere *is publishing (or has already published) an article on "Tracking Human Bootleggers," describing the traffic in smuggling aliens from Cuba into the United States.*

Years after the fact, I was embarrassed that I had written a letter with such chutzpah to Virginia Woolf. How could I have dared to tell her that her reasons for waiting to read my book while she finished hers were *splendid*? I was surprised that she even answered such a letter.

But she did answer it swiftly. It is the last of the three letters and was probably typed by Virginia Woolf herself, with eighteen corrections. Any secretary sending off a letter with so many typos and corrections would probably be fired. But of all the three letters, this is probably the most historically significant, for in it she reveals her agony in writing *The Years*, a book of frustrations, of lonely frustrated characters.

* * *

52, Tavistock Square, w.c.1.
Telephone: Museum 2621.

10th Jan. 1936

Dear Miss Gruber,
It is true that Christmas has come and gone and I had hoped to have done with my book. But unfortunately I was optimistic; and it won't be off my hands till March I fear. The last stages are always the most dreary; therefore I shall not attempt to read your study until my mind is free from this drudgery.
Many thanks for sending me the pamphlet. I am glad to know that you have been so successful. With best wishes for the new [sic] *Year,*

yours sincerely
Virginia Woolf

She was writing to me with even greater warmth than in her first letter, revealing her state of mind, her agitation. Leonard describes in his autobiography, *Downhill All the Way*, how ill she was at that time. "We had a terrifying time with *The Years* in 1936," he wrote. "She was much nearer a complete breakdown than she had ever been since 1913."

Then, in November 1936, she wrote in her diary,

I wonder whether anyone has ever suffered so much from a book as I have suffered from The Years.

After cutting the book drastically, she finally allowed it to be published in March 1937. It had the greatest success of any book she had written to that point.

My hours living with Virginia Woolf's work ended with this extremely revealing third letter. The typing was quavering; nearly every capital letter was out of line, almost unhinged; typographical errors were corrected with a stroke of a pen. Was she just then swinging into a depression? I read over and over her line to me that the last stages of writing a book are "always the most dreary" and she would finally read my book when her mind was "free from this drudgery."

Reading about her in Leonard's autobiography, I learned how depressed and agitated she became as she neared the end of nearly every book she was writing. She feared that the male critics would attack *The Years* and turned to Leonard for his critique. He tried to calm her by assuring her that the critics would love the book. But when the depression threatened her sanity, he packed her in their car and took her driving. Leonard, a skillful writer himself, a social and political activist, and responsible for the Hogarth Press, dropped everything to care for her whenever she became ill. She knew he was devoting his life to her, yet she referred demeaningly to him as "my Jew," and wrote a letter to a friend, saying, "I am marrying a poor, penniless Jew."

In a 1932 letter to Ethel Smyth, she described a birthday party for her Jewish mother-in-law and Leonard's nine brothers and sisters:

> *When the 10 Jews sat around me silently at my mother-in-law's, tears gathered behind my eyes, at the futility of life; imagine eating birthday cake with silent Jews at 11 p.m.*

She, like nearly everyone in her Bloomsbury circle, displayed what Nigel Nicolson had called "an occasional touch of anti-Semitism." Theirs was a British society rife with racism—racism against minorities, against people of color, and pointedly against Jews.

In these seventy years since I sat worshipfully in her parlor, I learned more of her violent manic depressions, her wild helpless swings; by turns critical, nasty, and catty, moving to exquisite warmth and generosity. I learned of her constant fear that she was going insane.

In 1941, when the pain of living finally had become too great for her, she wrote two final letters to Leonard before she walked into the river. He found one in her studio:

> *I want to tell you that you have given me the greatest possible happiness.*

He found the second one in their parlor. In it, she wrote even more lovingly:

Everything has gone from me but the certainty of your goodness. I can't go on spoiling your life any longer. I don't think two people could have been happier than we have been.

Those two love letters to Leonard, and her three letters to me, helped me work through my own anger and disillusionment, which now seem trifling in comparison to the agony she endured. They helped restore the admiration I had for her when I was nineteen and just discovering her genius. I realized that she had lived her entire life with a will to create as a woman. That was the most important lesson she had taught me. In 2004, I reread my dissertation in the light of that new understanding, underlining paragraphs that mean as much to me now as they did when I wrote them more than seventy years ago:

Virginia Woolf is determined to write as a woman. Through the eyes of her sex, she seeks to penetrate life and describe it. Her will to explore her femininity is bitterly opposed by the critics, who guard the traditions of men, who dictate to her or denounce her feminine reactions to art and life.

Admiringly, I described her literary integrity:

Against the critic, Virginia Woolf exhorts integrity, the Shakespearian 'To thine own self be true. . .'. Integrity for her [she writes in A Room of One's Own *], 'that integrity which I take to be the backbone of the writer lies in ignoring the critical admonishers and remaining inflexibly true to herself. . . . So long as you write what you wish to write, that is all that matters. . . .'*

Ruth Gruber
New York City
February 2005

HISTORICAL
DOCUMENTS

16th Dec 1931

Dear Madam,

Mrs Woolf has asked me to reply to your
letter about her books. I enclose a list of the books
published so far. I fear that I cannot give you a list
of articles &c published in periodicals, as there is
no list at present prepared.   For biographical facts
about Mrs Woolf, you could refer to Whos Who; or,
in a few weeks a study of Mrs Woolf's work and life
is appearing by Miss Winifred Holtby. This will give
all relevant facts about Mrs Woolf's life.

Mrs Woolf has always preferred to let her readers
decide for themselves as to the meaning of her books,
and therefore can not reply to your question as to
the autobiographical element in Orlando; but
it is generally known that the story is based, so far
as it is based on reality, on the life of Miss Sackville
West; and the house is understood to be Knole, the home
of Miss Wests ancestors in Kent.

Yours faithfully

P. Belsher

(Secretary)

Would you write direct to the Hogarth Press for
information about the essays by TS Eliot &c published
by them.

I arrived at Cologne University in 1931 on an Institute of International Education fellowship. A few weeks later, I was asked by Professor Herbert Schöffler to work for a Ph.D: "I have a special reason. I love Virginia Woolf's work. My students don't know English well enough to analyze it. You are the only American here. You would be writing the first doctoral thesis on her." I was flabbergasted. "My fellowship," I said, "is only for one year." "It's never been done in one year," he said, "but maybe you can do it." I hung VW's picture on my bedroom wall, and became mesmerized by her writing. *A Room of One's Own* became my bible, and *Orlando* my favorite novel. When I told Schöffler that I wanted to know much more about her, he suggested I write her at the Hogarth Press. Thus began my correspondence with her.

February 25, 1933.

TO WHOM IT MAY CONCERN:

We have found Miss Ruth Gruber to be exceptionally talented
as a translator, critic, and research worker. She is one of
those rare individuals who combines the intuitional grasp of
the artist with the calculating efficiency of the scientist.

Miss Guber has translated into English the German Classic,
"Das Edle Blut" by Wildenbruch. This book was published by
us in 1929 under the title, "Noble Blood," and has received
many flattering reviews from critics throughout the country.
Miss Gruber has read and criticized manuscripts and made
extensive researches for our editorial department.

Miss Gruber's work has been distinctive because she manages
to bring to it a greater degree of originiality than was
expected and produces a more complete and finished result
than was thought possible.

Very truly yours,

Barnes & Noble. Inc.

A. W. Littefield

awl/ec   Editor

In 1933, after returning home from Germany, I found a freelance job doing research and reading manuscripts for Barnes & Noble, then a small bookstore and publishing house near NYU. After a few weeks, they commissioned me to translate the German classic *Das Edle Blut*—*Noble Blood*—by Ernst von Wildenbruch into English. Hoping to help me find more work, the editor gave me this letter of introduction, which helped me find a few more literary jobs.

I was unbelieving when I received a letter from the Tauchnitz Press of
Leipzig, Germany—famous for printing classics by Charles Dickens and Jane
Austen and moderns like Virginia Woolf for English-speaking tourists—
informing me that they wanted to publish my Ph.D. dissertation on Virginia
Woolf. With apprehension and the chutzpah of youth, I sent this letter and
the green paperback, letter-press edition of my book to VW.

The Hogarth Press

52 Tavistock Square,   London,   w.c.1.   *Mus.* 3488.

Miss Ruth Gruber,   May 17th. 1935.
14 Harman Street,
Brooklyn,
New York,
U.S.A.

Dear Madam,

          Your letter of May 8th and the book to
which you refer, addressed to Mrs. Virginia Woolf,
have been received during her absence in Italy.
They will be placed before her on her return.

                    Yours faithfully,
                    THE HOGARTH PRESS.

                    Margaret West

                              MANAGER.

On May 17, 1935, this letter from the manager of the Hogarth Press, Margaret West, arrived in New York.

I had received a new fellowship to write a book on women under fascism, communism, and democracy. Since I was coming to Europe, I answered Ms. West's letter, and asked for an interview with Virginia Woolf.

Monk's House,
Rodmell, near
Lewes, Sussex.

June 21st 1935

Dear Miss Gruber,

I found your book waiting for me
on my return from Italy the other day.
I think that my secretary explained that
I was way--hence the delay in thanking you.
It was very good of you to send me a copy.
But I must confess, frankly, that I have not
read it, but I am sure you will believe
that this is not through laziness or lack of
interest in the subject. But the fact is that
I try to avoid reading about my own writing when
I am actually writing. I find that it makes me
self-conscious and for some reason
distracts me from my work.

But if I have not read it myself, I
have lent it to a friend, who is an
excellent critic; and I am told that you have
written a most sympathetic and acute study of
my books. I wixx shall read it as soon as I
have finished the book I am now working on.

I must thank you sincerely
for having taken this interest in my work.
That is in itself a great encouragement to me.
And I need not say how much I hope that
it will have a success with the public.

With thanks,

yours sincerely
Virginia Woolf

This was the first of the three letters that in 2004 turned up in one of my filing cabinets. It was written on June 21, 1935 from VW's home in Sussex. I never found out who the "excellent critic" was that found my book so sympathetic. Virginia Woolf mailed this letter on June 21 but I had left for Europe on June 22. My mother tucked it away in a file drawer for safekeeping. I did not see it until I returned home from traveling across Europe and the Soviet Arctic.

52 Tavistock Square London WC 1

12th Oct. 1935

Dear Madam,

I have only just received your
letter; and I am afraid that this will not
reach you in time.

I should of course be glad to do
anything I can to help you in your work;
and will arrnage to see you if possible. But
as I am not a politician and have no special
knowledge of the subject on which you are writing
I fear that it would probably be only a
waste of your time to see me.

If you like to ring up The Hogarth
Press Museum 3488 my secretary will
take a message. But as I say, I fear that
this letter will reach you too late.

Yours sincerely

Virginia Woolf

This was the second letter Virginia Woolf wrote me. It answered a letter I wrote her from Amsterdam for which I have no copy. It had its own strange odyssey. I had sent my letter to her from Amsterdam where I was visiting the Herz family with whom I had lived in Cologne. Virginia Woolf sent her answer to the Herz family in Amsterdam. They in turn had crossed out their address and redirected it to my address in Brooklyn. My mother stored it with the first letter in the same file drawer.

Mrs. Virginia Woolf
Monk's House
Rodmell, near
Lewes, Sussex

Dear Mrs. Woolf,

I thought this pamphlet showing the Arctic trip we discussed when I saw you last October in London might interest you.

I am wondering whether you have had time yet to read the study I made of your writings. Your reasons for waiting until you had finished your book were splendid, I thought. Now that Christmas has come, and I understood you to say that you would complete the work about Christmas time, I wondered if you had found the opportunity to read the work. I am deeply interested in your opinion of it.

With kindest regards to Mr. Woolf and yourself,

Yours sincerely,

P.S. It may interest you to know that the London News Chronicle published an article on the Arctic soon after I had spoken of it to you, and that the Sphere is publishing (or has already published) an article on "Tracking Human Bootleggers", describing the traffic in smuggling aliens from Cuba into the United States.

I wrote this letter to Virginia Woolf after she apparently sent me a letter I no longer have, saying she would read my book after Christmas. She hoped by then she would have finished the book she was writing; it was *The Years*.

52,
Tavistock Square,
W.C.1.
Telephone : Museum 2621.

10th Jan. 1936

Dear Miss Gruber,

It is true that Christmas has come
and gone, and I had hoped to have done with my book.
But unfortunately I was optimistic; and it wont be
off my hands till March I fear. The last stages are
always the most dreary; therefore I shall not attempt
to read your study until my mind is free from
this drudgery.

Many thanks for sending me the
pamphlet.   I am glad to know that you have been
so successful. With best wishes for the new
Year,
                    yours sincerely

                    Virginia Woolf

The last of the three letters seems to have been typed by Virginia Woolf
herself with eighteen corrections. In this letter she reveals her agony in
writing *The Years*, a book of frustrations for her.

Biographical Sketch

of

DR. RUTH GRUBER

"Upon the recommendation of the Fellowship Committee the Board of Trustees of the Federation awarded the fellowship of the Yardley Foundation for 1934-1935 to Dr. Ruth Gruber.

"At the age of fifteen Miss Gruber entered New York University and after three years received her Bachelor of Arts degree. She was awarded the La Frentz Fellowship to the University of Wisconsin, where she received her Master of Arts degree. The next year the Institute of International Education awarded her another scholarship to the University of Cologne, Germany, where she received her Ph.D. in one year, at the age of twenty, acclaimed the youngest doctor of philosophy in the world.

"Upon her return to America, Dr. Gruber devoted herself to literary work and public lectures. At the Newark Tercentenary observance of the birth of Spinoza, where the speakers included Consul General W. P. Montyn of Holland, Dr. Gruber gave the principal address. The Newark newspapers declared that 'her intellect, poise and subject matter fairly captivated her audience.'

"Touring the country on lecture tours, Dr. Gruber found material for articles which have appeared in various publications, including the *New York Times*. She has been foreign correspondent for newspapers in Germany and America.

"At present, as the Yardley Fellow, Dr. Gruber is writing a book on women in a changing world."

The New Jersey Club Woman.

To supplement my income during the Depression I began giving public lectures. This brochure was printed by a company that was helping me arrange bookings.

Women and the New Deal

●

Spinoza: God-intoxicated

●

The Rise and Fall of Women Through the Ages

●

Women Under Fascism, Communism
and Democracy

●

Virginia Woolf and the Will to Create
as a Woman

●

DR. RUTH GRUBER

is available for lectures on the above and related topics.
For further information, dates and fees,
communicate with

DR. RUTH GRUBER
14 HARMON STREET, BROOKLYN, N. Y.
Telephone: FOxcroft 9-8522

There were many topics I was prepared to speak on, especially "Virginia Woolf and the Will to Create as a Woman."

Comments by the American and European Press

"Ruth Gruber's return from the University of Cologne, Germany, with a Ph.D. *summa cum laude*, after a single year's residence, has aroused a great deal of admiring public attention; but one discovers no sign of surprise at its being a young woman, and not a young man, who has performed this extraordinary feat."

— *New York Evening Post* (Editorial: "Sex and Intellect"), September 18, 1932.

"She not only graduated with honors but at twenty years of age she is now the youngest Doctor of Philosophy in the world. Her professors are very enthusiastic about her achievement."

— *New York Times* (special cable), August 15, 1932.

"Dr. Gruber is the only student ever to be honored so young at the University of Cologne and the only one to win a doctor's degree in a single year."

— Anabel Parker McCann, *New York Sun*, August 29, 1932.

"Never before in the history of the University of Cologne has there been that distinction of according the doctorate to so young a student."

— *New York Times*, Rotogravure Section, Sunday, September 4, 1932.

"Young America paves the way through Dr. Gruber for the path which German students should follow."

— *Kölnische Zeitung*, July 30, 1932.

"A remarkable achievement is creating a flurry of excitement in university circles; an American student, Ruth Gruber, has broken all precedents at the University of Cologne."

— *General Anzeiger*, Bonn, July 31, 1932.

"The twenty-year-old American, Ruth Gruber, can claim the honor of being the youngest "Fräulein Doktor" ever graduated from a German University."

— *Berlin Tageblatt*, August 17, 1932.

"A young American, Ruth Gruber, who came to Germany on a Fellowship, has been awarded her Ph.D. at an age unrivalled by any native German."

— *Der Montag*, Berlin, August 15, 1932.

The brochure quoted from several articles that appeared after I returned home from Cologne, dubbed "the youngest Ph. D. in the world." Notwithstanding the publicity, I still couldn't find much work as the Depression took hold.

I was pleased that the brochure quoted the comments of the professors in Germany who had read my dissertation on Virginia Woolf, and other scholars and writers, such as the great novelist Lion Feuchtwanger.

Sissinghurst Castle, Cranbrook, Kent, TN17 2AB

Cranbrook (0580) 714239

31 Aug. 89

Dear Mr Lovell,

I've been in America, and only just got back to find your letter.

I think "a pure have yer" means "I've got you nailed, taped: you can't get out of seeing me" etc, like "Gotcha" (The Belgrano).

Dr Gruber won't be too pleased by this, but I was glad to read in VW's diary that she was quite flattered by what Dr. G. wrote about her in the earlier pamphlet, which was rare for Virginia

Yours sincerely

Nigel Nicolson

In this letter Nigel Nicolson explained the phrase Virginia Woolf had used before we met—"A pure have yer."

September 15, 1989

Mr. Nigel Nicolson
Sissinghurst Castle
Cranbrook
Kent , TN17 2AB

Dear Mr. Nicolson:

My good friend Aida Lovell has forwarded your
letter re Virginia Woolf to me. It was very kind
of you to send it.

I was beguiled by your explanation of
"a pure have yer" though I don't know what
"the Belgrano" in your letter means. And of course
I was delighted to discover from your note the following:
"I was glad to read in VW's diary that she was
quite pleased by what Dr. G. wrote about her in
the earlier   which was rare for Virginia."
Now I have searched in vain for this entry but
cannot find it. Would it be possible for you
to tell me where it appears in the diary?

My stepdaughter, Barbara Seaman, told me
she talked briefly with you after your lecture
in East Hampton this summer, and how much she
enjoyed it.

I hope I may hear from you again about
the Belgrano and the item in the diary.

Meanwhile this note takes you my gratitude
and my admiration for your work.

Sincerely,

In this letter I thanked Nigel Nicolson for writing to me.

25 September 1989

Sissinghurst Castle,
Cranbrook,
Kent TN17 2AB,
England

Dear Ms Gruber,

"A pure have yer". No wonder you were puzzled by my reference to the Belgrano. In the Falklands war the Argentinian cruiser, the Belgrano, was sunk by a British submarine with the loss of some 800 lives. Many of us thought this an act of needless butchery, specially as the cruiser was turning away from the Falklands towards her own home-port. But a terrible gutter-press newspaper here, called The Sun, came out with a photograph of the sinking ship under the 3-inch headline 'Gotcha'. This meant, in Cockney lingo, "Got you!". Considering that 800 Argentinian sailors had died, this was thought to be in the worst of taste (many of us thought the whole war was too).

So "a pure have yer" is comparable only for the slang - haveyer-Gotcha. It suggests a throw-away attitude, Cockney bravado, suggesting a task forced upon one which needs to be done.

As for Virginia being "quite pleased" with your pamphlet about her, I was referring to her diary of 31 May 1935. I fear that you may have been hurt by her references to you, but she was like that in her diary and letters, though perfectly courteous in conversation. It's one of the things I deplore about Virginia, her cattiness, contempt for almost everyone who were not her friends, an occasional touch of anti-Semitism, her snobbishness and jealousy. But it's almost heresy to suggest these things to the Virginia Woolf Society of the USA to whom she is Joan of Arc and Mother Teresa combined.

Yours sincerely,

Nigel Nicolson

Nigel Nicolson

Here Nigel Nicolson describes his feelings about Virginia Woolf. He is the sort of male critic that Virginia Woolf feared would dismiss her writing.

VIRGINIA WOOLF: A STUDY

BY RUTH GRUBER

KÖLNER
ANGLISTISCHE ARBEITEN

HERAUSGEGEBEN
VON
HERBERT SCHÖFFLER
O. Ö. PROFESSOR AN DER UNIVERSITÄT KÖLN

24. BAND:

RUTH GRUBER

VIRGINIA WOOLF A STUDY

LEIPZIG
VERLAG VON BERNHARD TAUCHNITZ
1935

VIRGINIA WOOLF
A STUDY

VON

RUTH GRUBER

LEIPZIG

VERLAG VON BERNHARD TAUCHNITZ

1935

Druck von Heinr. Pöppinghaus o. H.-G., Bochum-Langendreer

CONTENTS

Chapter One: The Poet versus the Critic   1

Chapter Two: The Struggle for a Style   8

Chapter Three: Literary Influences   23
                  The Formation of a Style.

Chapter Four: The Style Completed   38
                  And the Thought Implied.

Chapter Five: "The Waves" — the Rhythm of Conflicts   .   63

Chapter Six: The Will to Create as a Woman   .   .   77

THE POET VERSUS THE CRITIC

Virginia Woolf is determined to write as a woman. Through the eyes of her sex, she seeks to penetrate life and describe it. Her will to explore her femininity is bitterly opposed by the critics, who guard the traditions of men, who dictate to her or denounce her feminine reactions to art and life.

Seen through the struggle between poet and critic, a history of literature would appear as an endless conflict between two forces, one creating and one destroying. Dislocated by the War, modern literature is facing this conflict with desperate intensity. The literary world is torn between tradition and experiment. Poets defend themselves, critics their standards. Absolute values, in thought or style, become more than ever, esoteric and diffuse.

Of the contemporaries, Virginia Woolf is ordered within this struggle, evolving as she confronts it. Conscious of the forces against her, she molds herself in her poetic struggle for existence. Her problem is either that of adaptation, of accepting the protective standards of masculine critics, or of asserting her own identity and standing with heroic defiance, alone. In a confessional parenthesis, suggesting through an image the oppression, the "lash" of the critic, she acknowledges her struggle and its inevitable toll: "so cowardly am I, so afraid of the lash that was once almost laid upon my own shoulders." [1]

The blinding command "Thou shalt do this", the commandments of life or style which impel her to create, are distinguished as they are dictated by the critic or by her own poetic impulses. The professional critic, not the creative one, is acknowledged as he chooses or negates his poets, and establishes authoritative standards. The poet, not merely the maker of verse but the creative writer who can pour his vision into literary form, is acknowledged as he "consumes all impediments", [2] detaches himself from the critics, and creates molds standardized in turn by critics to come. The critic, seen as a menacing force, has two great means of impeding the poet: either by decrying him with arbitrary

---

[1] "A Room of One's Own" p. 136.
[2] Ibid. p. 88.

standards, throwing him into a state of doubt and struggle, and thereby, draining his imagination, or by offering him a crutch, which he swears has helped all the great poets of the past. In either, progress is aborted. The poets who fall victims to the critic, are of course the weaker ones, literature remaining the purer for their decease. Criticism becomes another form of wilderness temptation, destroying the unfit and maturing those who succeed against it. But for the young poet, still uncertain of his art, criticism, while vital, is most precarious. Struggling for a style, tasting and seeking literary influences before composing her early novels, Virginia Woolf apprehends this danger. Impressed by the wisdom of authority, she is conscious that not all traditions are despicable; that in the evolution of style, there has been a constant recurrence to the past. An unconditional submission to the critic, however authoritative, yet implies for her self-betrayal and poetic annihilation.

The critic, as he has been seen by poets from almost the beginning of stylistic time, is rarely presented in a flattering light. Personal grievances have made him a figure of either ridicule or baseness; the Simon Legree of literature. Only the deeper creative critics, like Pater or Wordsworth or Ruskin have done him justice, seeing in him the true arbiter, endowing him with the judicious, creative intelligence they perceive in themselves. Wordsworth, while he held no brief against the "Critic" as Virginia Woolf does in "Orlando", her satire of criticism, yet condemned that "numerous class of critics" who misunderstood him, and who "when they stumble upon these prosaisms, imagine that they have made a notable discovery, and exult over the Poet as over a man ignorant of his profession." [3] In "Orlando", the critic condemns not prosaisms but poeticisms, revealing a law of poetic action and critical reaction. With the persuasion of skill, the poets of one style become the most intolerant critics of the other.

The poet's complaint against the critic is probably as old as poetry itself. Speculation might surround even Homer with dissenters finding fault with his metaphors and his extravagant concepts of reality. Of the famous arguments against the critic, it is Fielding who denounces the whole race: "For a little reptile of a critic" to condemn "a great creation of our own . . . is a most presumptuous absurdity." [4] Lacking his masculine self-confidence, Virginia Woolf does not obliterate the critics so egregiously. Yet she resents their tyranny with as personal a grievance. She has allowed the truth of their condemnations too intimately to denounce them

[3] "Preface to the Lyrical Ballads" p. 19.
[4] "Tom Jones" Book X. p. 463.

in one blow as ignoramuses. Her method is more subtle: tracing critics from Elizabeth to the present reign of King George, she burlesques all their criticism in the same clichéd formula. Ironically, like a catechism for critics, comes the axiom: "marked by precious conceits and wild experiments." [5]

Against the critic, Virginia Woolf exhorts integrity, the Shakespearian "To thine own self be true . . ." She justifies the heroic poet who clings inexorably to his own judgment whether he be ridiculed or neglected by his generation. Although by their majority, critics and tradition and academies would appear to be the keepers of truth, and the poet with his single concept, deluded, she upholds this single concept, supported by the historical errors of the critics, as Gifford's negation of Keats. Integrity for her, "that integrity which I take to be the backbone of the writer" [6] lies in ignoring the critical admonishers and remaining inflexibly true to herself. In a lecture on women and fiction delivered to a women's college and expanded into the essay "A Room of One's Own", she sounds this cry for integrity. "So long as you write what you wish to write, that is all that matters . . . But to sacrifice a hair of the head of your vision, a shade of its colour, in deference to some Headmaster with a silver pot in his hand or to some professor with a measuring-rod up his sleeve, is the most abject treachery . . ." [7]

Only that writing impelled by inner necessity and modulated by her own "vision" has significance, whether that vision be the impulses of the woman, of the romanticist or the classic poet. Analyzed through the qualities she seeks in others, through the urgent truthfulness she demands from women, her own writing gains comprehension.

It is through the implicit peculiar vision of her sex, that she seeks to penetrate reality. The psychic consciousness of woman is her imperative medium. Her struggle for the "true" style and philosophy is determined not only by her own feminine impulses, but by her inheritance from the creative women who have preceded her. "We think back through our mothers if we are women" [8] as the thoughts of men are directed by Shakespeare and Napoleon and Christ. Like a feminine Stephen Dedalus, she seeks a spiritual mother from whom she can learn, and if possible, in herself surpass. Jane Austen, recently discovered by the moderns, by women especially like Katherine Mansfield, is for Virginia Woolf, of all poetesses, closest to Shakespeare. That will to remain true to her-

[5] "Orlando" p. 75; p. 236.
[6] "A Room of One's Own" p. 110.
[7] Ibid. p. 160.
[8] Ibid. p. 114.

self, to create as a woman, she seeks and discerns in the nineteenth century novelists, in Emily Brontë and Jane Austen. "What genius, what integrity it must have required in face of all that criticism, in the midst of that purely patriarchal society, to hold fast to the thing as they saw it without shrinking. Only Jane Austen did it and Emily Brontë. It is another feather, perhaps the finest, in their caps. They wrote as women write, not as men write. Of all the thousand women who wrote novels then, they alone entirely ignored the perpetual admonitions of the eternal pedagogue — write this, think that." [9]

She blames an aesthetic and moral break-down through adverse criticism for the poverty of great women writers in the past. Suggesting personal experience, she condemns the ubiquitous masculine critic as the negating force in their history. Women, she insists, must be allowed to dream their dreams after their own fashion; an intellectual emancipation is more vital than the vote. The past inferiority of women as creative writers she attributes to their long slavery, their subjugation to men. Like their minds, their writing was deformed in their struggle for freedom. The oblivion which has taken most of their work, she ascribes with trenchant self-analysis to the concessions they have made. Rebelling violently or defending themselves, the literary "mothers" sacrificed their objectivity beneath the critic's lash. "One has only to skim those old forgotten novels and listen to the tone of voice in which they are written to divine that the writer was meeting criticism; she was saying this by way of aggression, or that by way of conciliation. She was admitting that she was "only a woman", or protesting that she was "as good as a man". She met that criticism as her temperament dictated, with docility and diffidence, or with anger and emphasis. It does not matter which it was; she was thinking of something other than the thing itself. Down comes her book upon our heads. There was a flaw in the center of it .... She had altered her values in deference to the opinion of others." [10]

Beneath this analysis of the failure of women novelists, lies not only a personal observation, but the will to grow from the errors she has observed. Immortality is not insured by selling herself, as though the critic were a Mephistopheles grown respectable. From the bitter deception of momentary applause, she flees to the other extreme of desperate sincerity: "Praise and blame alike mean nothing." [11] And in her urgent cry for true self-expression, fame loses its immediate significance. Integrity alone is the great

---

[9] "A Room of One's Own" p. 112.
[10] Ibid. p. 112.
[11] Ibid. p. 160.

motto of her life: "So long as you write what you wish to write, that is all that matters, and whether it matters for ages or only for hours, nobody can say." [12]

Such integrity has its pitfalls. Fanatic blindness to all standards may be as destructive to the poet, as the lash of the critic. A Jane Austen, refusing to be told how to think, achieves greatness, not because she breaks all conventions, but because she adapts them to herself, circumscribing them in her own way. She does not shock the critics; she does not shake the laws of rhetoric to their roots. Rebelling, yet avoiding the extremes of fanaticism, she achieves quietly what the heroic Duchess of Newcastle sought in eccentricities. Violating nearly every custom she could touch, the Duchess wrote and philosophized when women were supposed to be pouring tea. Genius with its right to insanity, ruined her style, making it extravagant and grotesque. Signally for her own struggle against tradition, Virginia Woolf uncovers the Duchess' proclamation against the critic. In a veritable manifesto of integrity, the Duchess wrote, "I do not love to be led by the nose, by authority, and old authors; *ipse dixit* will not serve my turn. [13] The romanticism of such a character, breaking with a Napoleonic gesture, imperious literary bounds, appealed to Lamb's imagination. Like so many others whom Lamb had favored, the Duchess has a singular attraction for Virginia Woolf. Characteristically, she admires the Duchesses' "native wit, so abundant that outside succour pained it, so honest that it would not accept help from others." [14] But this honesty of wit, her extravagant integrity, led to purblinded egotism. She planned tremendous feats which she could never accomplish. In violent conflict with external forces and authority, she lost her stability and her judgment. Sensitive to such danger, Virginia Woolf deplores how "she became capable of involutions and contortions and conceits," [15] the pitfalls of integrity grown fanatic.

Between these two extremes, between exaggerated integrity and self-betrayal, Virginia Woolf attempts to steer her way. The course of being true to herself and yet admitting reasonable bounds, the course which Shakespeare and Jane Austen and Tolstoy had followed, she perceives to be the vital one for true creation. It is then that objectivity may be achieved, there being a freedom from inner struggle and outer rebellion. Analyzing the important problem of the mental state she considers "most propitious for creative work," she holds that it must be a mind which has risen

[12] Ibid. p. 160.
[13] "The Common Reader" p. 108.
[14] Ibid. p. 108.
[15] Ibid. p. 108.

above conflicts, "incandescent". "There must be no obstacles in it, no foreign matter unconsumed." [16] Shakespeare is her model, great because he has not made of his works confessional memoirs. Ill-concealed autobiography, lacking this incandescence, becomes sentimental and limited. Extravagantly subjective, such writing, Virginia Woolf holds, can never become immortal. Yet in defence of subjectivity lies Goethe's record that his works were "the fragments of a great confession". To Shakespeare's power of assimilating and thus concealing his conflicts, she ascribes his cause for greatness. "We are not held up by some revelation which reminds us of the writer. All desire to protest, to preach, to proclaim an injury, to pay off a score, to make the world the witness of some hardship or grievance was fired out of him and consumed. Therefore his poetry flows from him free and unimpeded. If ever a human being got his work expressed completely, it was Shakespeare. If ever a mind was incandescent, unimpeded . . . it was Shakespeare's mind." [17] That Shakespeare has risen serenely above conflicts is comprehensible to her; being a man, in a tradition of male poets, he could disregard the critics, whether they denounced him or grovelled at his feet. But only a "miracle" could endow Jane Austen, a woman, with such incandescence. "Here was a woman about the year 1800 writing without hate, without protest, without preaching. That was how Shakespeare wrote . . . and when people compare Shakespeare and Jane Austen, they mean that the minds of both had consumed all impediments; and for that reason we do not know Jane Austen and we do not know Shakespeare, and for that reason Jean Austen pervades every word that she wrote, and so does Shakespeare." [18] The great objectivity of their work she attributes not to the more obvious fact that little is known of their grievances, but to their ability to subvert their conflicts. The historical deficiency does not show her that if more were known of their lives, their readers could deduce what was hatred and what prejudice in their writing.

Upon this superb detachment, this critical harmony, she measures the greatness of her "spiritual mothers". Lady Winchilsea, Addison's contemporary, had fallen short in failing to obliterate her conflicts, to strike harmony with man. Distorted by her critical struggle, her mind was "harassed and distracted with hates and grievances. The human race is split up for her into two parties. Men are the 'opposing faction'; men are hated and feared, because they have the power to bar her way to what she wants

---

[16] "A Room of One's Own" p. 85.
[17] Ibid. p. 88.
[18] Ibid. p. 102.

to do — which is to write . . . Yet it is clear that could she have freed her mind from hate and fear and not heaped it with bitterness and resentment, the fire was hot within her." [19]

Vital for her conflict of tradition versus experiment, is the force with which Virginia Woolf is drawn to the women who repel literary influence. Originality, as the romanticists had conceived it, unreceptive and highly fitful, attracts her; she praises Charlotte Brontë because she "at least owed nothing to the reading of many books." [20] This freedom from traditions seems to have a paradoxical charm for Virginia Woolf in search of a maternal guide. Yet she blames this very "obstinate integrity" for the "flaw" in this "woman who . . . had more genius in her than Jane Austen." [21] Like almost every woman novelist, except Jane Austen, she was broken in the desperacy of her war with a masculine world. With her measurement of superb detachment, Virginia Woolf is persuaded that restless and unhappy, the novelist· Charlotte Brontë "will never get her genius expressed whole and entire. Her books will be deformed and twisted. She will write in a rage where she should write calmly . . . She will write of herself where she should write of her characters." [22] Lacking that serene objectivity, she fails because her art becomes too polemic, too subjective, too confessional.

The will for self-expression, whose frustration stifled the women of the past, Virginia Woolf pursues with renewed consciousness. Like her own analysis of Montaigne, she "wishes only to communicate (her) soul." [23] Free from unhealthful repression, to pour out the "poetry that is still denied outlet" in woman. [24] But what is this poetry, checked by the critics, and peculiar to women? What form does it have which makes it irrefutably feminine? Granted the traditional characteristics of woman, as her emotional rather than logical aspect of life, her strong sensitivities must find unimpeded expression. Hers must be a style molded to her feminine apperceptions, lyrical, poetic or diffusely narrative rather than constrained by strict laws of formal selectivity. A style supplying imagery for her associations and musical flowing rhythms for her emotions.

Obviously it is a style of pure romanticism. And several contradictions present themselves against a romantic style as uniquely feminine. First, women have shown that they are not all

---

[19] "A Room of One's Own" p. 88.
[20] The Common-Reader": "Jane Eyre" p. 223.
[21] "A Room of One's Own" p. 104.
[22] Ibid. p. 104.
[23] "The Common-Reader": "Montaigne" p. 96.
[24] "A Room of One's Own" p. 116.

emotional and obscurely associative. There are women rising up in science, in philosophy, in aesthetic criticism, who show a clarity and logic which repudiate all these feminine traditions. But such women, it may be argued, are not typical, at least for the contemporaries. With "masculine" mentality, their style becomes "masculine": abstract, structural and urgently clear. A rhythmic style would be anomalous. Since the traditional distinctions between man and woman, as the traditions of man's objective clarity and woman's irrational intuition still hold, these women must yet be crudely classified as masculine. An emotional romantic style in which most women can find truest expression, would still obtain as feminine. A deeper contradiction is derivative; this romantic style was created not by women but by men. Logically then, women seeking purely feminine expression, must reject it as most of them reject rigid formalism. But again the old traditions of what is masculine and what feminine are helpful; the men who created the romantic form, were, in their sensitivity and emotional attitude to life, more effeminate than manly. Having aptitudes similar to those of women, they perfected a "feminine" style which women could wield. It is no accident that the influence of women and their own creativeness appear far stronger in a romantic epoch than in a classic or naturalistic one. It is there that they find deepest expression, deepest sympathy.

Under the law of polarity, of poetic action and critical reaction, this feminine style is negated by a correlative "masculine" criticism, demanding a verisimilitude in the treatment of life, a denial of metaphors used only as ornament, and a prose which is neither metrical poetry nor the monotonous jargon of a legal code. Such criticism, following the naturalists and the classicists, and characteristically convinced that it alone has found the absolute truth in style, rejects this feminine romanticism as sentimental and pretentiously emotional. It substitutes for women's rhapsody, restraint; for their rhythms, apparently bald or logical structure; and for their dreams, tangible reality.

Within this polarity, Virginia Woolf struggles for her style, conscious that it has broken other women before her.

THE STRUGGLE FOR A STYLE

The problem of style which has concerned Virginia Woolf, reflects, with deepened intensity, the speculative problems of aesthetics. Vacillating reactions from poetic romanticism to terseness and objectivity, are as indigenous to her conflicts and progress as they are to a literary age. She is driven to break her forms as soon as she has created them. Her experiments, her variations and recurrences reveal not only the urge to discover new possibilities, but a deeper discontent and lack of assurance. The lyrical cry, echoed throughout her works, faint at times, at others swelling relentlessly, evinces an ebb and flow of self-confidence, of doubt, of attempted change, and grim resolution.

In the irreconcilable alteration from her first novel, "The Voyage Out" to "Night and Day" her second, the lash of masculine criticism seems to have fallen. Where she rollicked in her first novel, she criticizes in her second. The rebellion of youth, the desire to be unrestrained by critical traditions is suppressed. In bending to the critic and evading future stings, she endangers her original beliefs, her original style, her integrity as a creative woman. She attempts to subvert her poetry into prose and her images into facts. She becomes ratiocinative like the critics themselves. She writes slowly and thoughtfully where before she had loosened herself in the torrent of poetic soaring and youthful love.

The change in her style looms large in the change in her heroines, in the women who interest her. Rachel of "The Voyage Out" is a dreamer, fantastic, musical, in love with Beethoven and Bach. Her romantic flights from reality, her lyrical feminine character find their setting on board the ship "Euphrosyne," breaking its way through the eternity of water and air. Landed in a distant English island, Rachel's antisocial appetencies, her love of solitude are developed in a microcosmic society of vacationists and pioneers who have voyaged out. With tragic fatalism, she falls in love with a would-be novelist and is torn between sacrificing either her identity or her love. The conflict seems insoluble; death resolves it. Even her death is fitting to her personality in its fever, its delirium, its romantic hallucinations.

On the other hand, Katherine Hilberry of "Night and Day" emerges mathematical, scientific, precise. Her life is spent in bringing order and precision into the chaos of a poetic house. Again love creates the conflict; but in her reflective logic, she finds the happiness denied Rachel. Sensible, unruffled by passions, restrained, she consents to marry a man whom she does not love, but who offers her intellectual freedom. Analytic to the end, she finally ascertains where completion for her lies, and marries the poor lawyer, Denham, whom she loves. Between the two women, as between the two novels, lies a difference in observations, in reactions, in a concept of life, comprehended in their style.

The writing of the first, immature novel with its reverberation of poetic feminine imagery, of rhythmic cadences, of words highly charged with suggestion, is reminiscent of the Romantic Victorians. The simple "like" images, as in Ruskin, fall almost invariably at the end of the sentence to create a satisfying cadence, viz:

"At this point the cab stopped, for it was in danger of being crushed like an egg-shell." [1]

"The argument was spilt irretreviably about the place like a bucket of milk." [2]

"The inside of his brain was still rising and falling like the sea on the stage." [3]

"Relics of humour still played over her face like moonshine." [4]

"The world floated like an apple in a tub." [5]

Analyzed, such figures recall associations of simple phenomena in nature, or, as the "apple in a tub", of childhood games and discoveries. They show a feminine poetic identity with nature, and lack sophisticated allusions to psychology, literature or the other arts. Their naïveté would verify the Schopenhauer definition of woman's childishness. The longer metaphors, being less restrained, realize a peculiar feminine imagery, with the rhythm and tonal diction of lyrical verse.

"She was more lonely than the caravan crossing the desert; she was infinitely more mysterious, moving by her own power and sustained by her own resources. The sea might give her death or some unexampled joy, and none would know of it. She was a bride going forth to her husband, a virgin unknown of men; in her vigour and purity, she might be likened to all beautiful things, for as a ship she had a life of her own." [6]

That the boat "might be likened to all beautiful things" seems an acknowledgement of a vagueness in her sensation of beauty; a vagueness which she does not qualify either because

---

[1] "The Voyage Out" p. 6.
[2] Ibid. p. 34.
[3] Ibid. p. 80.
[4] Ibid. p. 79.
[5] Ibid. p. 80.
[6] Ibid. p. 29.

her mind lacks one definite objectified image, (a feminine tradition,) or she is conscious that her associations, as that of the ship as a virgin, are literary pickings, unassimilated.

Through unusual comparisons, she blocks out her characters in this early novel. The comic figures, like Mr. Pepper, a misanthropic bibliophile, are described figuratively, with the domestic associations of an observant, quick-witted woman.

"His heart's a piece of old shoe leather." [7]

"He's like this," said Rachel, "lighting on a fossilised fish in a basin, and displaying it." [8]

"They saw Mr. Pepper as though he had suddenly loosened his clothes, and had become a vivacious and malicious old ape." [9]

Or Mr. Dalloway, the politician, weighing the social ameliorator against the artist, is described with feminine minuteness, in sleep. "He looked like a coat hanging at the end of a bed; there were all the wrinkles, and the sleeves and trousers kept their shape though no longer filled out by legs and arms. You can then best judge the age and state of the coat." [10] Even the tragic figures, like Rachel, are characterized metaphorically. Seasick, where her "sensations were the sensations of potatoes in a sack on a galloping horse", she had "just enough consciousness to suppose herself a donkey on the summit of a moor in a hail-storm, with its coat blown into furrows; then she became a wizened tree, perpetually driven back by the salt Atlantic gale." [11] Revealing both a poetic and feminine mentality, this early imagery of donkeys and galloping horses is curiously reminiscent of the nursery with wooden toys, its walls or its illustrated story books. The desire to remain unsophisticated, finds expression, often unconsciously, in associations of childhood. The return to nature in literary art implies a retrogression even beyond puberty; only the child is untainted, being least removed from natural innocence. Virginia Woolf's spontaneous imagery draws largely from this native childish consciousness. But in reverting from nature to literary sources, her images become less plastic and more abstract, tending to grow forced or intellectual or cryptically obscure.

By their very nature, associations usually lack exactitude, the crucible of "masculine" criticism. It is a curious commonplace that as the mind matures, it recoils from vague suggestions, however pictorial, and demands a more literal truth. This individual change is but a reflection of the evolution of the race, expressing itself first

---

[7] "The Voyage Out" p. 14.
[8] Ibid. p. 13.
[9] Ibid. p. 11.
[10] Ibid. p. 68.
[11] Ibid. p. 78.

in carving or scribbling images, and then in words so limited and absolute that they can be compiled within a standard dictionary. Writing her first novel in the language of poetic youth, Virginia Woolf, through a desire for progress or through critical pressure, converts her style, and writes her second novel in the language of ratiocination, with little imagery and less rhythm.

Her style in "Night and Day" is suggestive partly of the restraint of a Jane Austen, and especially of the intellectual periods of a poet like Wordsworth or Coleridge, writing in prose. A brilliancy of color and of sound is restrained; there is a conscious attempt to write prosaically, denying emotional outbursts. A sober logic marks the whole, typified ingeniously in the heroine, who "preferred the exactitude, the star-like impersonality, of figures to the confusion, agitation, and vagueness of the finest prose." [12] Apparent in this sentence lies Virginia Woolf's analysis of her own conversion; she is maturing, demanding dictionary values; her early prose, however sincere, has become vague and unsatisfying to her.

The difference in these two styles, a difference in accepted feminine and masculine expression, is vividly portrayed by a comparison of the first paragraphs of both novels. An involuntary self-consciousness in the author makes the early pages of a book almost an inevitable standard for the complete work. The predominating style, if it has been at all premeditated, is generally characterized here and most easily disintegrated. The mold is set; its limitations and its potentialities are conspicuous; the sentence structure and the atmosphere are strongly apprehended with their suggestion of imagery, rhythm, tone-color or stoic restraint. In "The Voyage Out" the first few pages leap in their action, with traditional feminine irrelevancy, from one surprise to another. In emotional suggestive diction, mysterious hints of a possible quarrel between husband and wife are enclosed in Ruskinian rhythms, droll didacticisms, imagery, and poetic, wandering observations.

"As the streets that lead from the Strand to the Embankment are very narrow, it is better not to walk down them arm-in-arm. If you persist, lawyer's clerks will have to make flying leaps into the mud; young lady typists will have to fidget behind you. In the streets of London where beauty goes unregarded, eccentricity must pay the penalty and it is better not to be very tall, to wear a long blue cloak, or to beat the air with your left hand.

"One afternoon in the beginning of October when the traffic was becoming brisk a tall man strode along the edge of the pave-

---

[12] "Night and Day" p. 40.

ment with a lady on his arm. Angry glances struck upon their
backs . . . But some enchantment had put both man and woman
beyond the reach of malice and unpopularity . . .

"The embankment juts out in angles here and there, like
pulpits; instead of preachers, however, small boys occupy them,
dangling string, dropping pebbles, or launching wads of paper for
a cruise. With their sharp eye for eccentricity, they were inclined
to think Mr. Ambrose awful; but the quickest witted cried
'Bluebeard!' as he passed . . .

"Although Mrs, Ambrose stood quite still, much longer than
is natural, the little boys let her be. Some one is always looking
into the river near Waterloo Bridge; a couple will stand there talking for half an hour on a fine afternoon; most people, walking
for pleasure, contemplate for three minutes; when, having compared the occasion with other occasions, or made some sentence,
they pass on. Sometimes the flats and churches and hotels of
Westminster are like the outlines of Constantinople in a mist;
sometimes the river is an opulent purple, sometimes mud-coloured,
sometimes sparkling blue like the sea . . . Then there struck close
upon her ears —
> Lars Porsena of Clusium
> By the nine Gods he swore —

and then more faintly, as if the speaker had passed her on his
walk —
> That the Great House of Tarquin
> Should suffer wrong no more." [13]

The lyrical feminine tone permeating the novel is definitely
set here, in the colorfulness of the diction, in the strength of the
verbs of action and the vivid adjectives. Feminine too are the
profuse observations, the comparisons and the musical rhythm.
But in her second novel, the language becomes denotative rather
than suggestive, the sentences involved and architecturally con-
structed. In place of the melodic "opulent purple" and the
romantic "outlines of Constantinople in a mist" are such Latinities
as "unoccupied faculties" and "unmitigated truth."

"It was a Sunday evening in October, and in common with
many other young ladies of her class, Katherine Hilbery was
pouring out tea. Perhaps a fifth part of her mind was thus occupied, and the remaining parts leapt over the little barrier of day
which interposed between Monday morning and this rather subdued moment, and played with the things one does voluntarily and
normally in the daylight. But although she was silent, she was

---

[13] "The Voyage Out" pp. 1—3.

evidently mistress of a situation which was familiar enough to her, and inclined to let it take its way for the six hundredth time, perhaps, without bringing into play any of her unoccupied faculties . . . .

"Considering that the little party had been seated round the tea-table for less than twenty minutes, the animation observable on their faces, and the amount of sound they were producing collectively, were very creditable to the hostees." [14]

Feminine imagination is not obliterated, but is self-consciously guarded. An attempt to confine herself to facts is striking after the associative flights of "The Voyage Out." There, grief, the grief of a mother had been depicted in short native Anglo-Saxon idioms with rhythmic graphic imagery. "What with misery for her children, the poor, and the rain, her mind was like a wound exposed to dry in the air." [15] Three words, "misery", "children" and "exposed", in the whole cadenced sentence deviate from the monosyllabic pattern. Grief in "Night and Day" is no longer the emotional grief of a mother, but the intellectual grievance of a lawyer at odds with his environment. Comparatively analyzed, its expression is devoid of sentiment and imagery, slowly deliberative. "He tried to recall the actual words of his little outburst, and unconsciously supplemented them by so many words of greater expressiveness that the irritation of his failure was somewhat assuaged. Sudden stabs of the unmitigated truth assailed him now and then . . ." [16]

There is a maturity in such writing which unveils the reversion from the bubbling, overflowing expressiveness common to youth. Here Virginia Woolf denies her arbitrary associations; the "true" style lies in a more factual reality than her lyrical imagination imposes. Yet a complete suppression of the earlier poetry is impossible; traces of her former imagery and rhythmic romantizations appear, suggesting that they are more native to her than the stoic adherence to logic and objectivity. Objects are no longer unquestionably like something else, but the "smaller room was *something* like a chapel in a cathedral, or a grotto in a cave, for the booming sound of the traffic in the distance *suggested* the soft surge of waters, and the oval mirrors, with their silver surface, were like deep pools trembling beneath starlight." [17] The lyric, feminine romanticism has returned only to be

14 Night and Day" pp. 1—2.
15 "The Voyage Out" p. 5.
16 "Night and Day" p. 16.
17 "Night and Day" p. 7.

shattered directly by a cold analysis of the imagery. "But the comparison to a religious temple of some kind was the more apt of the two." [18] A defined reaction against emotional creativeness is conspicuous; she is seeking like the Joyceans and the humanists, anti-sentimentality and restraint.

Apologetically, she tries to justify her effeminate, romantic impulse for illusions, for conceits. "To put it figuratively", becomes the excuse. The world is no longer a delightful vision, "like an apple in a tub", but "a good world, although not a romantic or beautiful place or, to put it figuratively, a place where any line of blue mist softly linked tree to tree upon the horizon." [19] Her poetic urge to associate, to explain one sensation through another, seems irrepressible, yet she gives it a new form, distorted under apologies.

In the mentality of her characters, she personifies her conflict between rhapsody and pragmatic restraint. The sentimental exuberance of youth she encloses in Cassandra, (the very name is typical), and in Mrs. Hilberry, daughter of a poet. But in Katherine, her daughter, she personifies mature sobriety. Seen through one of the characters, descriptions of beauty are allowed; loveliness is no longer the observation of the author. A dinner table, always an object of ornamental worship for Virginia Woolf, is suffered here only through Cassandra's vision. "Had the scene been looked at only through her eyes, it must have been described as one of magical brilliancy." [20] But her pleasure in the refulgent patterns and colors "must be repressed", Virginia Woolf decrees ironically, conscious of the restraint she is teaching herself, "because she was grown up and the world held no more for her to marvel at." [21] Yet the poetess consoles herself; if she has forsaken the world of mysterious wonders, of woods and fairies and breathless sensations, she has found a new world, profounder in its broader scope. Life, reality, human beings have taken the place of fanciful illusions. "The world held no more for her to marvel at, it is true; but it held other people, and each other person possessed in Cassandra's mind some fragment of what privately she called 'reality'." [22] Cassandra does not lose her romantic spirit of wonder, but diverts it from fascinating flowers or poems to fascinating human beings. She retains her exuberance in expressing this new fixation, while Virginia Woolf seeks, less

[18] Ibid.
[19] Ibid. p. 379.
[20] Ibid. p. 365.
[21] Ibid.
[22] "Night and Day" p. 365.

naturally, to adapt an intellectual form to her psychological interest in man. The idea, the Platonic concept, stands now as the impetus of life, with God or love or nature. The poet has matured into the philosopher. It is Katherine who embodies this newly evolved mode. "What is it that makes these people go one way rather than the other? It's not love; it's not reason; I think it must be some idea. Perhaps . . . our affections are the shadow' of an idea. Perhaps there isn't any such thing as affection in itself . . ." [23]

If the change in her style be the inevitable result of a profound conversion in her concept of life, it would signalize maturity rather than a loss of integrity, or doubt. But the self-consciousness of this new tone, the startling echoes of the earlier lyricism and its apologetic concessions, suggest that she has come to this style while she is still in conflict. She has neither obliterated her poetry nor ascertained the beauty of unrhythmic prose. Where before, imagery and tone were an integral part of her writing, she has now become uneasily style-conscious. She is wary of purple prose, and speaks of it with abstract or learned criticism. She disintegrates conceits from her style and analyzes their value. With quizzical irony, she makes Rodney, the poet of classical formalism, read a scientific paper on the use of metaphors in Elizabethan poetry. "It had been crammed" she derides it "with assertions that such-and-such passages, taken liberally from English, French, and Italian, are the supreme pearls of literature. Further, he was fond of using metaphors which, compounded in the study, were apt to sound either cramped or out of place as he delivered them in fragments. Literature was a fresh garland of spring flowers, he said, in which yew-berries and the purple nightshade mingled with the various tints of the anemone; and somehow or other this garland encircled marble brows." [24]

The vague impossible associations of overwrought purple prose, observed in herself, she condemns in him. She has assumed, with doubtful integrity, the compensating role of destructive critic; having denied the poetry in herself, she begins to criticize it in others. But her criticism is not bitter. She is still too uncertain of her new convictions to laugh devastatingly at the old. She has still not taken an absolute stand; her mind has not "consumed impediments" and become "incandescent". She wavers between denying, or giving expression to her romantic femininity and emotional hallucinations. It is the tortuous problem which

[23] Ibid. p. 287.
[24] "Night and Day" p. 49.

she later satirizes in "Orlando", detailing her struggle and
solution. With acute insight, her travesty is that of a man laughing
at himself. She mocks with no injured hatred of the world, no
polemics, no fear of retaliation. In portraying her own conflict,
she has objectified it. "Orlando" seems as much the history of her
own literary growth as that of Miss Sackville-West or of England.
Virginia Woolf appears to trace her poetic development from that
of a romantic child to a woman seeking the realities modulated
by her sex.

The primary impulse of her youth, which is the urge to
write, she depicts in Orlando, "a nobleman afflicted with a love of
literature." [25] The parallel is close, Virginia Woolf being a noble-
woman by birth, the daughter of the essayist, Sir Leslie Stephen.
Mocking the creative urge, she analyzes her concept of literary
style. "It was the fatal nature of this disease to substitute a phan-
tom for reality" [26] definitely the romantic concept of writing.
Style becomes the expression of a personal illusion rather than of
absolute, objective truth.

Just as Monsieur Rolland had attempted to set down the
processes by which his hero created, and succeeded in showing
himself more than Jean Christophe in the flux and reflux of
inspiration, so Virginia Woolf depicts the struggle with which she,
like Orlando, "undertook to win immortality against the English
language." [27] With obvious intimations of self-characterization,
she confesses that "Anyone moderately familiar with the rigours
of composition will not need to be told the story in detail; how
he wrote and it seemed good; read and it seemed vile; corrected
and tore up; cut out; put in; was in ecstasy; in despair; . . .
vacillated between this style and that; now preferred the heroic and
pompous; next the plain and simple; now the vales of Tempe; then
the fields of Kent or Cornwall; and could not decide whether he
was the divinest genius or the greatest fool in the world." [28]

His style is a burlesque upon her own. He experiences the
same conflict of impulsive romantic writing against the restraint
produced by destructive criticism. And like Virginia Woolf,
maturity awakens him to the reality beyond his imagination. Imagery, profuse in her early writing is, with conscious
travesty, wild and unconstrained in his. Making love to a Russian
princess, he calls her "a melon, a pineapple, an olive tree, an
emerald, and a fox in the snow all in the space of three seconds;

---

[25] "Orlando" p. 62.
[26] "Orlando" p. 62.
[27] Ibid. p. 69.
[28] Ibid.

he did not know whether he had heard her, tasted her, seen her, or all three together." [29]

Both Orlando and Virginia Woolf are essentially visual-minded, and aural in their sensitivity to life's rhythm. "Sights disturbed him," she says of Orlando, "sights exalted him — the birds and the trees; and made him in love with death, the evening sky, the homing rooks; and so, mounting up the spiral stairway into his brain-which was a roomy one — all these sights, and the garden sounds too, the hammer beating, the wood chopping, began that riot and confusion of the passions and emotions which every good biographer detests." [30] She seems not only to be classifying her own faults but even chastising herself. The young Orlando is not a clear worshipper of the eye, desiring to see objects in their structural truth. The eye for Orlando is only the quick passage between the object and his imagination, his memory and his consciousness. He goes to nature to satisfy his need for beauty, but he perceives this beauty only through the associations it has stimulated. The beauty of a tree lies not in its tangibility, but in its likenesses; in its strange outline against the horizon or its wavering reflection in a stream. The fantastic shapes cast by nature suggest images of wildest romanticism. "Trees were wooded hags, and sheep were grey boulders." [31] Orlando "likened the hills to ramparts, to the breasts of doves, and the flanks of kine ... compared the flowers to enamel and the turf to Turkey rugs worn thin." [32] In the same manner that she had satirized Rodney's confusion of conceits in "Night and Day", Virginia Woolf now mocks Orlando's. "Images, metaphors of the most extreme and extravagant twined and twisted in his mind." [33]

Partly inspired in its title and Elizabethan imagery by Robert Greene's fragmentary play, "The History of Orlando Furioso" (ca. 1591) "Orlando" takes its hero from Shakespeare to the present, and in all ages, shows the struggle for integrity, the struggle between the poet and the critic. At the hands of Nick Greene, modelled perhaps from the author of the "Orlando Furioso", Robert Greene the Shakespearian critic, satirist and pamphleteer, Orlando suffers a poet's torments. In her reverberating accusations against the aesthetic or social critic, Virginia Woolf endangers her objectivity, her crucible of artistry. In her essays, where she is defending or propounding a thesis, objectivity is less vital than in her novels. She meets the danger however, in this fantastic

---

[29] Ibid. p. 31.
[30] Ibid. p. 13.
[31] "Orlando" p. 121.
[32] Ibid. p. 121.
[33] Ibid. p. 31.

satire of criticism, by mocking not only critics but poets as well. If she accuses her own oppressors, she laughs too at their victim. The conceits which mark Orlando's poetry are a travesty upon all romantic imagery. Reality lies only in his imagination, to which he gives wild expression. He is happy, untormented, so long as he writes in solitude. But the moment he shows his work to the critic, his stability is gone. Nick Greene, symbol of the critic of all ages, denounces his style as "wordy and bombastic" [34] and holds his allegorical metaphors up to ridicule. Orlando's desire to create, greater than all else in life, is mutilated. Philosophy, friendship and even nature cannot console him. He wavers between the reality he perceives and the new standard set by the critic. He cannot bring himself to write as Nick Greene would dictate. Yet the criticism of his own style, with its pathetic fallacies, has stung him deeply. He is oppressed by the ominous conflict, observed in Virginia Woolf, the conflict of rationalization and poetic emotion. His images, he is told, are not truthful; he is wildly rhapsodic; he has no idea of objective reality, of "Life".

He attempts to change his style. Integrity hangs in the balance. " 'Another metaphor by Jupiter!' he would exclaim . . . 'And what's the point of it?' he would ask himself. 'Why not say simply in so many words —' and then he would try to think for half an hour, — or was it two years and a half? — how to say simply in so many words what love is. 'A figure like that is manifestly untruthful', he argued, 'for no dragon-fly, unless under very exceptional circumstances, could live at the bottom of the sea'." [35] He is beginning to seek the truth beyond his imagery, and in condemning conceits, he consciously adopts even the language of ratiocination. "Manifestly", "under very exceptional circumstances", these are Latinities which before would have made him shudder. But it is all for truth, and to the professor, truth lies in polysyllables. So he rejects his vision of the dragon-fly because it lacks scientific veracity. " 'And if literature is not the Bride and Bedfellow of Truth, what is she? Confound it all', he cried, 'why say Bedfellow when one's already said Bride? Why not simply say what one means and leave it?' So then he tried saying the grass is green and the sky is blue to propitiate the austere spirit of poetry whom still, though at a great distance, he could not help reverencing. 'The sky is blue', he said, 'the grass is green'. Looking up, he saw that, on the contrary, the sky is like the veils which a thousand Madonnas have let fall from their hair,

---

[34] Ibid. p. 80.
[35] "Orlando" p. 84.

and the grass fleets and darkens like a flight of girls fleeing the embraces of hairy satyrs from enchanted woods." [36]

Under cover of mock biography, Virginia Woolf thus gives expression to the desperate struggle of poetic versus critical realism, of rhapsody versus restraint. For Orlando at least, solution is hopeless. "I don't see that one's more true than another. Both are utterly false." [37] Orlando had known no such dilemma before acknowledging the critic. His feelings alone in the early songs of innocence had guided him to what was true and what was false. Truth had been emotional, a simple sensation; the critic, bringing experience and self-analysis, makes it involved, an intellectual perception. His dreams are called hollow, his visions, quixotic. Orlando loses first the self-confidence and then the sincerity of a Shakespeare or a Jane Austen to see life as he chooses. He begins to fall prey to tradition. He wavers, he looks about him for props, he wonders what "a true poet, who has his verses published in London, would say about the grass and sky." [38] The lash, almost laid upon Virginia Woolf's shoulders, is now laid heavily upon his. He cringes to the critic, to Nick Greene, as though Nick "were the Muse in person." [39] He exposes his creations desperately, offering the critic "a variety of phrases, some plain, others figured." [40] But the critic with his eyes cast on Cicero and the "Gloire" of the past, discourages all his attempts whether they be in his old style or his new. And suddenly Orlando sees the light — "I'll be blasted if I ever write another word, or try to write another word, to please Nick Greene or the Muse. Bad, good, or indifferent, I'll write, from this day forward, to please myself." [41] Integrity has conquered and "Orlando" takes its place in the long procession of works "In Defence of the Poet Against the Critic".

The poetry which Virginia Woolf had repressed in "Night and Day" she burlesques here as that romantic, effeminate poetry which revelled in Lorelis and in dark cavernous landscapes. With a few devices to make these extravagant visions seem Orlando's, she holds no check upon her own fancy. "What woman," she gushes, "would not have kindled to see what Orlando saw then burning in the snow — for all about the looking-glass were snowy lawns, and she was like a fire, a burning bush, and the candle flames about her were silver leaves; or again, the glass was green water, and she a

[36] Ibid. p. 85.
[37] Ibid. p. 86.
[38] Ibid. p. 87.
[39] "Orlando" p. 87.
[40] Ibid. p. 87.
[41] Ibid. p. 87.

mermaid, slung with pearls, a siren in a cave, singing so that oarsmen leant from their boats and fell down, down to embrace her." [42] The tone of "Orlando" is one of arch belittling; the humor is heightened by the very apologies and modifications which in "Night and Day" suggest an aesthetic breakdown, a self-conscious concession to the critic. The luminous color and mystic Pre-Raphaelite images, derived from Virginia Woolf's own fancy and typical of her feminine creation, are attributed with droll satire to Orlando. "Now the Abbey windows were lit up and burnt like a heavenly, many-coloured shield (in Orlando's fancy); now all the west seemed a golden window with troops of angels (in Orlando's fancy again) passing up and down the heavenly stairs perpetually." [43]

She apologizes humorously, not only for her extravagant images but for her connotative diction. Made conscious of her feminine flair for associations, she seeks to justify herself with sincerity. Thus letting Orlando fling himself under an oak tree, she justifies the extravagance in the word "flung", through a hyphenated apology: "— there was a passion in his movements which deserves the word —." [44]

In satirizing Orlando, she gives vent to all the lyricism, all the sentimental illusions she had repressed in herself. The onrush of thoughts and words is typical of the liberation of her style. The color and tremendous movement felt here, she repeats throughout the book; the abundance of her visions swells the length of her sentences, and to give them all expression, she reverts to the medieval device of lists. The pure pleasure in words incites such a profusion of kaleidoscopic details that her sentences seem to rock with the burden of single completed visions. In purple rhythms with long lists of swaying verbs: she describes how the lights "dipped and waved and sank and rose, as if held in the hands of troops of serving men, bending, kneeling, rising, receiving, guarding, and escorting with all dignity indoors a great Princess alighting from her chariot." [45]

Her style-consciousness reveals to her the danger of incoherence in this rich hurling together of words and images. After a long winding exposition of the incongruities and mysteries in nature, that "the poet has a butcher's face and the butcher a poet's," or "we know not why we go upstairs, or why we come down again", she breaks her form, and with the personal intrusion of a romantic essayist, acknowledges not only "the perhaps

---

[42] Ibid. p. 157.
[43] Ibid. p. 45.
[44] "Orlando" p. 16.
[45] Ibid. p. 17.

unwieldy length of this sentence", but the feminine confusion of unassimilated images in her mind: "a piece of policeman's trousers lying cheek by jowl with Queen Alexandra's wedding veil." "A perfect rag-bag of odds and ends within us," [46] is her jocular self-analysis.

Through the medium of healthy humor, she has found herself. In laughing at her conflict, she has risen above it. She perceives that there is truth in each phase of it, that romanticism is not a deeper stylistic experience than realism, or that material fact is not more absolute than the imagination. It is only in ascertaining where, by natural impulses, she belongs, that she can write with the integrity implicit in greatness. The doubt which she satirizes in Orlando after wavering miserably between "plain and figured phrases", she has herself experienced, like almost every poet Orlando, as a Victorian woman, loses confidence in her vision and style; oppressed by critical standards, she turns to other writers in perplexity. "Here came by a pair of tight scarlet trousers — how would Addison have put that? Here came two dogs dancing on their hind legs. How would Lamb have described that? For reading Sir Nicholas and his friends . . . they made one feel — it was an extremely uncomfortable feeling — one must never, never say what one thought . . . They made one feel, she continued, that one must always, always write like somebody else . . . and though I'm spiteful enough, I could never learn to be as spiteful as all that, so how can I be a critic and write the best English prose of my time?" [47] With a violent "Damn it all!" she overturns the influence of the critic and determines to give expression to the realities she has discovered. "Enforcing upon herself the fact" — a fact which Virginia Woolf acknowledges through all her later works and repeats almost literally in the essay "Mr. Bennett and Mrs. Brown" "that it is not articles by Nick Greene on John Donne nor eight-hour bills nor covenants nor factory acts that matter; it's something useless, sudden, violent; something that costs a life; red, blue, purple; a spirit; a splash; like those hyacinths (she was passing a fine bed of them); free from taint, dependence, soilure of humanity or care for one's kind; something rash, ridiculous, like my hyacinth, husband I mean, Bonthrop: that's what it is — a toy boat on the Serpentine, ecstasy — it's ecstasy that matters." [48] She is driven to this decision by the strength of her natural impulses. She returns to that early state of romantic exuberance, of feminine intuition and a dreamy nature-worship. Typifying the Victorian roman-

[46] Ibid. p. 66.
[47] "Orlando" p. 242.
[48] Ibid. p. 245.

ticists, Orlando now revels in night and moonlight, where sensuous objects grow indistinct and intangible visions seem to usurp the deeper reality. "Night had come — night that she loved of all times, night in which the reflections in the dark pool of the mind shine more clearly than by day." [49] Orlando has struggled between light and darkness, between romanticism and reality, certain now that darkness is her native realm. At last she can give unrestrained expression to the poetry singing within her. She obliterates the critic and his attempt to expose this darkness as a world of shadowy creations, which fall like ghosts before a penetrating searchlight.

When, in integrity, Orlando achieves greatness, she weighs the long sought-for external success with her own impulses, her need for self-expression. "What has praise and fame to do with poetry? Was not writing poetry a secret transaction, a voice answering a voice?" [50] She has experienced the greatest happiness possible to the idealistic poet, "the voice answering the voice", poetry for its own sake, poetry for communication and self-expression. It is this revelation, which now suffuses Virginia Woolf. "Orlando" appears as a great confession of its author's struggles and her realization of clarity and peace. It lacks that complete objectivity, that detachment of self which she thinks to find in Shakespeare or Jane Austen. But Virginia Woolf does not lose herself in violence or condemnation. If she is bitter against the critical Nick Greene, avenging herself upon the critics who have attempted to impede her, she ridicules Orlando too. Her ability to laugh at herself has saved her from destruction or despair. Through a humorous though profound self-analysis, she has absolved herself from struggles. She has achieved that psychic stability which subdues restlessness and eliminates revolt. Writing with the power of persuasion, she can stand above all constrictions, serenely impervious. Like Orlando, she cringes no longer to critics; periods of doubt and perplexity, recurring inevitably perhaps, she has learned to hold under check. While not insolently deaf to criticism and dissent, she has ascertained the style in which she finds complete ease for expression. As a woman and a dreamer, she gives vent to her imagination, repressing not her visions but a vagueness in expressing them. She has not lost her fire, but learned to control it, possessing eloquence without bombast, imagery without becoming extravagant or fatiguing.

[49] Ibid. p. 276.
[50] Ibid. p. 274.

LITERARY INFLUENCES:
THE FORMATION OF A STYLE

The danger in choosing literary influences, Virginia Woolf perceives, conscious that the great stylists of the past have in the main been men. The woman novelist cannot return only to the women of the past. It is in the men, in the poets and the masculine rhetoricians, that she is taught to seek her molds. However feminine Virginia Woolf's aspect of life may be, her form is still precariously influenced; she must still confine herself within the frame which man has built for his own needs, the frame of the novel, the lyric or the drama. Even her selection of a form apparently adaptable to woman, the novel, necessitates concession. Having found in the history of style no artistic cast which was irrefutably feminine, she is forced, within womanly restrictions, to accomodate herself to man's peculiarities, to his diction and the structure he created for his thoughts and emotions.

To maintain her integrity, her poetic womanhood, she selects those men as literary influence whose style woman can wield with least constraint. Characteristically, she studies not the classical Attic writers but the Asiatic ones; not Dryden but Burke or Gibbon; not Pope but Shelley.

A style is analyzed as it is the consummation of those which have preceded it. Even the sportive or revolutionary experiments are evaluated as reactions to tradition and only then comprehended in their singularity. That not only muffled traces of the great stylists of the past appear in Virginia Woolf's novels, but direct citations and arguments in their defence, is an instrumental consideration of her writing. Her motive, like the traditional artist, is to recreate these influences, manifesting then with what integrity or conscious plagiarism she has schooled herself.

Fresh from the lecture hall, or the advice of tutors, she is, in her first novel, most obviously colored by masculine and academic influence. Gibbon, Burke, Shelley, Milton, Wordsworth and Shakespeare are discussed, debated, admired and defended. Gibbon, a master of the grand style, she envies with the homesickness of a modern who believes perfection to lie dead in the past. "A whole procession of splendid sentences" [1] from the "Decline and Fall", she visions as flawless soldiers, entering Hirst's "capacious brow . . . marching through his brain in order . . . until the entire regiment had shifted its quarters." [2] Rachel is to

[1] "The Voyage Out" p. 121.
[2] Ibid. p. 121.

be educated to understand Gibbon, since most women lack either the training or the ability. A typical passage is even quoted from him, characterizing his flowing technigue. It is a trait enviably sought by Virginia Woolf in her early formation of a style. Rachel, reading the book beneath a tree "with a feeling that to open and read would certainly be a surprising experience, . . . turned the historian's page and read that. —

"His generals, in the early part of his reign, attempted the reduction of Aethiopia and Arabia Felix. They marched near a thousand miles to the south of the tropic; but the heat of the climate soon repelled the invaders and protected the unwarlike natives of those sequestered regions . . .

"Never had any words been so vivid and so beautiful — Arabia Felix — Aethiopia." [3] Her appreciation, her emotional analysis of the Victorian stylist, is significant for Virginia Woolf's early inclinations. In her enthusiasm for names with musical alliteration, she shows a distinct romantic heritage. She attempts to imitate the musical device used by Poe in "Ulalume", by giving the characters in this first novel, liquid names like Rachel Vinrace, Helen, Evelyn, Terence, and Clarissa — a reminiscence of that earlier Richardson figure of utter feminine sentimentality. Her romanticism reaches its peak in the name of the ship "Euphrosyne". As she develops, the names of her characters grow curiously less romantic and in her last novel, the "Waves", are as uneuphonious, as solid, as Susan, Jinny and Rhoda.

As she grows more certain of her style, she no longer mentions the literary giants as though she were defending them before an iconoclastic world or repeating the admiration schooled in her. She uses other writers largely to suggest the personality of the character who admires them. William of "Night and Day" precise, fastidious, with a flair for classic formulas, reads Pope. Ralph, his converse, a natural talent and informed in plants and flowers, reads Sir Thomas Browne. Long quotations, as that from Gibbon in her first novel, decrease into a few lines from the poets, especially from Shelley or Shakespeare. Her interest in a model prose style, implicit in the rhetorical masters, disappears as conversation from her novels, and demanding expression, becomes material for essays. Her novels then are freed from the oppression of literary dogmatism. In "The Common Reader" a collection of her essays, she gives vent to her admiring concern for the writers who have in some way influenced her; for Chaucer, Addison, Defoe, Montaigne, the Duchess of Newcastle, Jane Austen, the Brontës, George Eliot, Conrad, and Sophocles, for "it is to the Greeks that we turn when we are sick of the vagueness, of the

[3] "The Voyage Out" p. 205.

confusion, of the Christianity and its consolations, of our own age." [4] The sort of appreciative propaganda which characterized her first novel, is assimilated slowly as she matures. Hints of it are still apparent in "Night and Day". She insinuates an indirect defence of Dostoievsky, whose "Stavrogin's Confession" she has translated, by having Rodney exhort the romantic Cassandra "to read Pope in preference to Dostoievsky, until her feeling for form was more highly developed." [5] Shakespeare is not only defended by Mrs. Hilberry, a poetic Victorian, but she conceives a project of making him public property. With street corner propaganda, she will lower him from the exclusive aristocracy of the critics and make him common good. "I should like to stand at that crossing all day long and say: 'People, read Shakespeare!'" [6]

Burke's influence is felt in the careful selectivity of her diction, gaining suggestive power by its rhythm, its tone and its compositional relationship. A description, reminiscent of his purple prose, effects its colorfulness at times through a strict adherence to the objects described, and at others through metaphorical associations.

"When the Spaniards came down from their drinking, a fight ensued, the two parties churning up the sand, and driving each other into the surf. The Spaniards, bloated with fine living upon the fruits of the miraculous land, fell in heaps; but the hardy Englishmen, tawny with sea-voyaging, hairy for lack of razors, with muscles like wire, fangs greedy for flesh, and fingers itching for gold, despatched the wounded, drove the dying into the sea, and soon reduced the natives to a state of superstitious wonderment . . . From the interior came Indians with subtle poisons, naked bodies, and painted idols; from the sea came vengeful Spaniards and rapacious Portuguese; exposed to all these enemies (though the climate proved wonderfully kind and the earth abundant) the English dwindled away and all but disappeared." [7]

The Asiatic flush of this description is gained through the stylistic devices which she has learned from the male rhetoricians, the finesses of balancing, of parallel construction, and triads. Comparing it with Burke's famous description of the horrors of Hyder Ali, reveals a resemblance not only in the machination, but in the rhythmic rise and fall and the sustained rapidity of motion.

---

[4] "The Common Reader": "On Not Knowing Greek" p. 59.
[5] "Night and Day" p. 295.
[6] Ibid. p. 323.
[7] "The Voyage Out" p. 101.

"Then ensued a scene of woe, the like of which no eye had seen, no heart conceived, and which no tongue can adequately tell. All the horrors of war before known or heard of were mercy to that new havoc. A storm of universal fire blasted every field, consumed every house, destroyed every temple. The miserable inhabitants, flying from their flaming villages, in part were slaughtered; others without regard to sex, to age, to the respect of rank or sacredness of function, fathers torn from children, husbands from wives, enveloped in a whirlwind of cavalry, and amidst the goading spears of drivers, and the trampling of pursuing horses, were swept into captivity in an unknown and hostile land. Those who were able to evade this tempest fled to the walled cities; but escaping from fire, sword, and exile, they fell into the jaws of famine." [8]

Burke's unusual denotation of the word "compounding" in his illustrious sentence: "compounding all the materials of fury, havoc, and desolation into one black cloud" [9] has become a constant in her active vocabulary. She repeats the borrowed word in the mold of triads in which Burke had set it: "The power is a mysterious one compounded of beauty, birth, and some rarer gift." [10]

Other words made memorable by some poet or famous prose writer, are accepted synthetically in her work. "Innumerable", a favorite of Wordsworth's and of the romantic poets, suggests to her such liquid rhythm that she constructs euphuistic balance by doubling it repeatedly.

"The housemaids, the innumerable housemaids, the bedrooms, the innumerable bedrooms." [11]

"Innumerable beadles were filling innumerable keys into well-oiled locks." [12]

"Her ears were now distracted by the jingling of innumerable bells on the heads of innumerable horses." [13]

Echoes of the early grammars she has studied, with their tabulated lists of connotative and denotative diction, their models of rhetorical perfection, persist from her earliest novel to her latest.

Just as famous words of literature become synthetic in her style, so famous phrases are wholly incorporated, given only a slight turn for originality. Milton's "Sonnet on his Blindness" is appropriated to "the thought of that one gift which it was death to hide — a small one but dear to the possessor — perishing and with it my self, my soul." [14] Stevenson's confession of having "played

---

[8] "Speech on the Nabob of Arcot's Debts" p. 7.
[9] Ibid. p. 6.
[10] "Orlando" p. 106.
[11] "Mrs. Dalloway" p. 29.
[12] "A Room of One's Own" p. 21.
[13] "Orlando" p. 232.
[14] "A Room of One's Own" p. 57.

the sedulous ape" is converted into "the ape is too distant to be sedulous." [15] Shelley's "Stanzas Written in Dejection near Naples":

> "I could lie down like a tired child,
> And weep away the life of care"

are literally repeated in her last novel "The Waves". "I am not going to lie down and weep away a life of care," [16] while various lines now "classic" from T. S. Eliot's "The Love Song of J. Alfred Prufrock" appear throughout all her later novels.

> "Should I, after tea and cakes and ices,
> Have the strength to force the moment to its crisis?"

suggests a similar thought in "The Waves". "Now let me try . . . before we rise, before we go to tea, to fix the moment in one effort of supreme endeavour." [17] Or "Prufrock's" last image

> "I have seen them riding seaward on the waves
> Combing the white hair of the waves blown back".

is startlingly recalled in "Jacob's Room": "and life became something that the courageous mount and ride out to sea on — the hair blown back." [18]

Her manner of adapting these literary influences reveals a significant feature of her work. Deeply style-conscious, hers is a style founded upon wide reading, upon a study of the classicists with the determination to learn from them and find patterns for her own writing. Her method is not only that of recreating but of direct imitation, either conscious or unconscious. Where it is conscious, as the Miltonic reproduction, her imitation is mainly for the sake of effect. The great men need no correction; repeating their thought, she repeats also their expression. Whether these thoughts and their related form are peculiarly masculine or peculiarly feminine here does not concern her; they are the deep truths of life, and if a man has given them perfect expression, she is willing to accept this masculine mold. Where her influences become subconscious, as the influence of Burke, they form for the most part the groundwork of her own personal style. But where they are unassimilated, as the images from T. S. Eliot, they appear almost to be plagiarisms, modified by slight individuality.

With a curious repudiation of her own literary influences, she dissuades women from the masculine stylists whom she herself has invoked. "It is useless to go to the great men writers for help, however much one may go to them for pleasure. Lamb, Browne,

---

[15] Ibid. p. 114.
[16] "The Waves" p. 166.
[17] Ibid. p. 41.
[18] "Jacob's Room" p. 251.

Thackeray, Newman, Sterne, Dickens, De Quincey — whoever it may be — never helped a woman yet, though she may have learnt a few tricks of them and adapted them to her use." [19]

Yet her own first two novels are indelibly the product of her masculine studies; she has done far more than simply "learnt a few tricks" from Lamb and Sir Thomas Browne. She repudiates men as teachers for the modern woman writer only after her conscious search for influences is ended. She speaks with experience of the dangers in imitating a style alien to her womanhood.

As in a picture gallery, Virginia Woolf draws literary portraits of all the men whom she has studied. Imitating their styles in her key work "Orlando", she describes their appearance from Elizabethan England to the present. Like Joyce's "Ulysses", she makes the prodigious attempt to trace the history of style in English literature. Yet though she owes much of her inspiration to Joyce, she cannot parody as he does. Her irony is not devastating enough; she is still too reverential to laugh at the figures she admires. Her vision is too brightly colored by her own personality; she cannot reproduce styles alien to hers, as Pope's or Swift's. At best, she recalls the Elizabethans, with whom modern English style, after Chaucer, begins. With brilliant insight, she satirizes their profusion of metaphors, their flair for allegory and their flowery "inspired" style, perceiving in them the traits in her own youthful writing. In discussing the danger of meditation, she gives vent to a torrent of bombastic associations which pale their minor Elizabethan models.

"It is these pauses (of reminiscences) that are our undoing. It is then that sedition enters the fortress and our troops rise in insurrection. Once before he had paused, and love with its horrid rout, its shawms, its cymbals, and its heads with gory locks torn from the shoulders had burst in. From love he had suffered the tortures of the damned. Now, again, he paused, and into the breach thus made, leapt Ambition, the harridan, and Poetry, the witch, and Desire of Fame, the strumpet; all joined hands and made of his heart their dancing ground." [20]

Immature writers are largely attracted to warfare as a possibility for conceits. The noise and furious movement stimulate them as they stimulate a people not of necessity barbaric or childish, yet not highly intellectual. As imagery, these flourishes of war often become repellently inflated, recalling romantic associations fallen into sad repute. Such stale visions are amusing

---

[19] "A Room of One's Own" p. 114.
[20] "Orlando" p. 68.

in "Orlando", being exaggerated for the sake of parody and humor; but that Virginia Woolf's travesty of the Elizabethan conceits is founded upon her own style, is evidenced in similar passages in her more serious novels. "She was laughed at", she writes in "To the Lighthouse", "fire-encircled, and forced to vail her crest, dismount her batteries, and only retaliate by displaying the raillery and ridicule of the table" [21] all because she had proposed cleaner dairies.

Lyly's "Euphues and his England" is suggested in its artifice of balance of similar phrases and parallel construction. That she has studied him for a time at least is probable, though he, far more than the Elizabethans, is an influence which seems to have become subconscious.

"At length, however, there was no room in the galleries for another table; no room on the tables for another cabinet; no room in the cabinet for another rose-bowl; no room in the bowl for another handful of potpourri; there was no room for anything anywhere; in short the house was furnished." [22]

The monotonous evenness of such euphuistic phrases with identical molds, whose rhythms are varied only by a new though slight thought, is even supplemented by the tripping tone implicit in Lyly. It is followed by a descriptive list whose length and discursive similarity seems to vie with Chaucer or the "Romaunt of the Rose".

"In the garden snowdrops, crocuses, hyacinths, magnolias, roses, lilies, asters, the dahlia in all its varieties, pear trees and apple trees and cherry trees and mulberry trees, with an enormous quantitiy of rare and flowering shrubs, of trees evergreen and perennial, grew so thick on each other's roots that there was no plot of earth without its bloom, and no stretch of sward without its shade." [23]

Sir Thomas Browne's style is suggested too, though with too much reverence to be called parody. She repeats his diction consciously and recalls his rhythm and philosophy of life:

"But of all that killing and campaigning, that drinking and love-making, that spending and hunting and riding and eating, what remained? A skull; a finger. Whereas, he said, turning to the page of Sir Thomas Browne, which lay open upon the table — and again he paused. Like an incantation rising from all parts of the room, from the night wind and the moonlight, rolled the divine melody of those words which, lest they should outstare this page, we will leave where they lie entombed, not dead, embalmed

---

[21] "To the Lighthouse" p. 160.
[22] "Orlando" p. 93.
[23] "Orlando" p. 93.

rather, so fresh is their colour, so sound their breathing — and Orlando, comparing that achievement with those of his ancestors, cried out that they and their deeds were dust and ashes, but this man and his words were immortal." [24]

The parallel with the "Hydriotaphia: Urn-Burial" is obvious not only in the language but in the concern with immortality. The passage recalls, with marked similarity, the famous sentences in the fifth chapter: "Had they made as good provision for their names as they have done for their relics, they had not so grossly erred in the art of perpetuation." [25] The seventeenth century philosopher's flair for the word "diuturnity" recurs again, with unmistakeable influence, in "Orlando". "Of the two forces which alternately, and what is more confusing still, at the same moment, dominate our unfortunate numbskulls — brevity and diuturnity — Orlando was sometimes under the influence of the elephant-footed deity, then of the gnat-winged fly." [26] The identical thought appears in Sir Thomas Browne, though his style here is more intellectual than is Virginia Woolf's. "And therefore restless inquietude for the *diuturnity* of our memories unto present considerations, seems a vanity almost out of date, and superannuated piece of folly." [27]

The transition in literary periods is made more obviously in "Orlando" than in "Ulysses". Joyce changes from one completed style to another without explanation; the styles develop integrally. In "Orlando" literary time is always recited, Virginia Woolf being its discursive annotator. In a running commentary, she shows the change in writing:

"For it is for the historian of letters to remark that he (Orlando) had changed his style amazingly. His floridity was chastened; his abundance curbed; the age of prose was congealing those warm fountains. The very landscape outside was less stuck about with garlands and the briars themselves were less thorned and intricate." [28]

The eighteenth century is heralded in; the style is discussed rather than parodied or, as with Sir Thomas Browne's, reproduced often unconsciously. With feminine, romantic lawlessness, she tells what she, as an interpreter, thinks about the poets, what she feels about their styles and mannerisms. Pope's style

[24] Ibid. p. 68.
[25] Urn-Burial" p. 115.
[26] "Orlando" p. 84.
[27] "Urn-Burial" p. 116.
[28] "Orlando" p. 95.

is not suggested through clever imitation, but she analyzes it like a critical biographer herself, and as in her Gibbon quotation, cites him directly. It is a less sophisticated and less artistic method than Joyce's, but it recalls significantly her own standards of creative criticism. With her ubiquitous complaint against the critics, she seeks comprehension for the poet himself. "In short, every secret of a writer's soul, every experience of his life, every quality of his mind is written large in his works, yet we require critics to explain the one and biographers to expound the other." [29] Here one of the direct intentions in "Orlando" becomes apparent; it appears as a satire of the contemporary biographical urge which she ridicules in the essay "Mr. Bennett and Mrs. Brown" as "those portentous and ridiculous biographies, that milk-and-watery-criticism." [30] Her consciousness of biographies is derived perhaps from her father, Leslie Stephen and from Lytton Strachey, a member of the "Bloomsbury group" to which she belongs, and which includes Clive Bell, E. M. Forster and Duncan Grant. Yet like the "Stürmer und Dränger" she seeks meaning only in the poet and not in his sterile commentators. His character, his mannerisms, his humor as well as his philosophy, she probes intuitively in his writing, and recreates the dead poet for herself. "The temptation", she writes in "The Common Reader", "to read Pope on Addison, Macaulay on Addison, Thackeray on Addison, Johnson on Addison rather than Addison himself is to be resisted." [31]

Denouncing the critical commentators, Virginia Woolf assumes their role herself, seeking the deep "human interest" which characterizes Lytton Strachey's biographies. Sensitive to aesthetic form she brings to the style of the poets, the same creative criticism she has used in analyzing their characters. Again in the manner of the historical biographer, she describes the change in the style of the eighteenth century. Orlando, now a woman, goes to school to Pope and Addison and Swift:

"They were very witty, too (but their wit is all in their books), and taught her the most important part of style, which is the natural run of the voice in speaking — a quality which none that has not heard it can imitate, not Greene even, with all his skill; for it is born of the air, and breaks like a wave on the furniture, and rolls and fades away, and is never to be recaptured, least of all by those who prick up their ears, half a century later, and try. They taught her this, merely by the cadence of their

---

[29] Ibid. p. 177.
[30] "Mr. Bennett and Mrs. Brown" p. 28.
[31] "The Common Reader": "Addison" p. 139.

voices in speech; so that her style changed somewhat, and she wrote some very pleasant, witty verses and characters in prose." [32]

Her method of showing literary influences wavers between the Strachey method of commentation and Joyce's method of imitation. The period of restrained Attic prose, she discusses; that of Asiatic purple prose, she imitates. Echoes of De Quincey are unmistakeable in Orlando's conversion from man to woman, though in time, this being the dawn of the eighteenth century, the style is premature. But the Opium Eater is well chosen to depict the fantastic vision of a man changed physically into womanhood. De Quincey's melodic rhythms are recalled, his allegory and symbolism are literally copied.

"The doors gently open, as if a breath of the gentlest and holiest zephyr had wafted them apart, and three figures enter. First, comes our Lady of Purity; whose brows are bound with fillets of the whitest lamb's wool; whose hair is as an avalanche of the driven snow; and in whose hand reposes the white quill of a virgin goose. Following her, but with a statelier step, comes our Lady of Chastity; on whose brow is set like a turret of burning but unwasting fire a diadem of icicles; her eyes are pure stars, and her fingers, if they touch you, freeze you to the bone. Close behind her, sheltering indeed in the shadow of her more stately sisters, comes our Lady of Modesty, frailest and fairest of the three; whose face is only shown as the young moon shows when it is thin and sickle shaped and half hidden among clouds. Each advances towards the centre of the room where Orlando still lies sleeping; and with gestures at once appealing and commanding, 'Our Lady of Purity' speaks first . . ." [33] The three ladies are echoes of De Quincey's vision in his "Dream-Fugue", and such melancholy rhythms as "grief and lamentation" are taken directly from his style:

"The eldest of the three is named 'Mater Lachrymarum', — Our Lady of Tears. She it is that night and day raves and moans, calling for vanished faces. She stood in Rama, when a voice was heard of lamentation — . . .
"Her head, turreted (the very word repeated in Virginia Wolf's parody) like that of Cybele, rises almost beyond the reach of sight . . . Madonna moves with uncertain steps; fast or slow, but still with tragic grace. Our Lady of Sighs creeps timidly and stealthily. But this youngest sister moves with incalculable motions, bounding and with a tiger's leaps. She carries no key; for, though coming rarely among men, she storms all doors at which she is permitted to enter at all. And her name is 'Mater Tenebrarum' — Our Lady of Darkness." [34]

---

[32] "Orlando" p. 180.
[33] "Orlando" p. 113.
[34] "Dream-Fugue" p. 50.

To trace the poet Orlando through the ages of literature required a degree of sexual flexibility; there were periods, the Elizabethan, for example, when women were only to be sung to; they themselves had no voices. In order for Orlando, living through the sixteenth century, the Restoration and the era of the Metaphysical poets, to be a typical poet, he was forced to be a man. But how account for his turning woman in the Age of Englightenment, when poets were still virile? Virginia Woolf may have been thinking of Lady Winchilsea or even more of the Duchess of Newcastle, to whom Orlando bears conscious resemblance, in her flair for conceits, for allegory, and her speculations on the nature of integrity and womanhood. But the Duchess was a contemporary of Jeremy Taylor and Sir Thomas Browne, writing at a time when Orlando is still portrayed in his masculinity. It is curious that Virginia Woolf did not choose the nineteenth century for Orlando's conversion, when Jane Austen and the Brontës were gaining quiet recognition, and Dorothy Wordsworth was helping her brother under no great obscurity. She may have been experimenting with history, speculating that "Elizabethan literature would have been very different from what it is if the woman's movement had begun in the sixteenth century and not in the nineteenth." [35]

In describing Orlando's character as a woman, Virginia Woolf satirizes the contents of "Lady Chatterley's Lover". Lawrence's belief that love is the prime motif in a woman's life, and sex the most fitting subject for a novel, is burlesqued in a direct travesty of Lady Chatterley's affair with her gamekeeper.

"And when we are writing the life of a woman, we may, it is agreed, waive our demand for action, and substitute love instead. Love, the poet has said, is woman's whole existence . . . Surely, since she (Orlando) is a woman, and a beautiful woman, and a woman in the prime of life, she will soon give over this pretence of writing and thinking and begin at least to think of a *gamekeeper* (and as long as she thinks of a man, nobody objects to a woman thinking). And then she will write him a little note (and as long as she writes little notes nobody objects to a woman writing either) and make an assignation for Sunday dusk and Sunday dusk will come; and the gamekeeper will whistle under the window — all of which is, of course, the very stuff of life and the only possible subject for fiction." [36]

Creative imitation reaches its heights in the scene in which

---

[35] "A Room of One's Own" p. 152.
[36] "Orlando" p. 227.

Orlando is "safely delivered of a son". De Quincey is once more recalled with Ruskin and the late Victorian poetic prose writers.

"Hail! natural desire! Hail! happiness! divine happiness! and pleasure of all sorts, flowers and wine, though one fades and the other intoxicates; and half-crown tickets out of London on Sundays, and singing in a dark chapel hymns about death, and anything, anything that interrupts and confounds the tapping of typewriters and filing of letters and forging of links and chains, binding the Empire together . . . Hail, happiness! kingfisher flashing from bank to bank, and all fulfillment of natural desire, whether it is what the male novelist says it is; or prayer; or denial; hail! in whatever form it comes, and may there be more forms, and stranger. For dark flows the stream — would it were true, as the rhyme hints 'like a dream' — but duller and worser than that is our usual lot; without dreams, but alive, smug, fluent, habitual, under trees whose shade of an olive green drowns the blue of the wing of the vanishing bird when he darts of a sudden from bank to bank . . .

"But wait! but wait! we are not going, this time, visiting the blind land. Blue, like a match struck right in the ball of the innermost eye, he flys, burns, bursts the seal of sleep; the kingfisher; so that now floods back refluent like a tide, the red, thick stream of life again; bubbling, dripping; and we rise, and our eyes (for how handy a rhyme is to pass us safe over the awkward transition from death to life) fall on — (here the barrel-organ stops playing abruptly).

" 'It's a very fine boy, M'Lady', said Mrs. Banting, the midwife, putting her first-born child into Orlando's arms. In other words Orlando was safely delivered of a son on Thursday, March the 20th, at three o'clock in the morning." [37] The influence of Joyce's Lying-in-Hospital scene in "Ulysses" seems likely. The device of invocations is repeated, as well as the midwife's announcement that the child is born and of the much desired sex.

"Send us, bright one, light one, Horhorn, quickening and wombfruit. Send us, bright one, light one, Horhorn, quickening and wombfruit. Send us, bright one, light one, Horhorn, quickening and wombfruit.
Hoopsa, boyaboy, hoopsa! Hoopsa, boyaboy, hoopsa! Hoopsa, boyaboy, hoopsa!" [38]

The contemporary post-Joyceian flair for coining new words, built upon the ruins of the old, or formed only for the association of sound, holds little interest for Virginia Woolf. She prefers the well traditioned word-images of the earlier stylists to

[37] "Orlando" p. 249.
[38] "Ulysses" p. 150.

the revolutionary inventions of Joyce and the "Transition" writers, contributors to an experimental magazine which reached its heights in 1927—28. Only once does she imitate them and then so archly that her "Rattigan Glumphoboo" appears as jocular contemporary satire. Orlando, telegraphing to her husband in an excitement of almost mad incoherence, wires in the style of "Ulysses'" last chapter: "life literature Greene toady Rattigan Glumphoboo." [39] Omitting all verbs and adjectives, it is the associational, topical language of the subconscious, which Joyce had popularized and which Virginia Woolf defines as a "cypher language" conveying "a whole spiritual state of the utmost complexity." [40] Satirizing this experimental writing, Virginia Woolf again annotates: "it cannot have escaped the reader's attention that Orlando was growing up — which is not necessarily growing better — and 'Rattigan Glumphoboo' described a very complicated spiritual state —." [41] The stylistic time has become the present.

Not only the history of literary influences is portrayed in "Orlando" but traces of all the styles in which Virginia Woolf has composed and is yet to experiment, are suggested and developed. The romantic, imaginative, emotionally feminine writing, discerned in her first novel, is parodied in Orlando's early style. His conversion to "plain phrases" recalls the attempted restraint of "Night and Day" where Virginia Woolf had sought to express a profundity of thought in a structural logic. "Orlando" itself, the mock biography, follows in the footsteps of Lamb and the subjective, tongue-in-their-cheek, romantic essayists. Hints of the stream-of-consciousness, explored in the later novels appear in Orlando's constant reminiscences of the past. Impressionism is suggested in the kaleidoscopic description, the flashes of rapid completed observations. "Orlando" is thus seen not only as the final acknowledgement of Virginia Woolf's literary influences, but as the core of her own stylistic development.

An analysis of literary influences is incomplete, almost fruitless, unless it solves the consequent problem of originality, the problem which every poet sets himself. A complete repudiation of influences is, considering Shakespeare's borrowings, absurd. The masterful artist is known by the influences he selects, by the unwavering certainty with which he finds the influences he needs and converts them to his own use. Essentially it is the crisis of the literary apprentice, forced to determine when, for his own

---

[39] "Orlando" p. 241.
[40] Ibid. p. 239.
[41] Ibid. p. 240.

identity, he must free himself from adulation. With her reverence for the great masters, Virginia Woolf faces the problem precariously. Her first two novels appear as the trial and error stage of her development, the tasting and probing. Uncertainly, she accepts and rejects both traditions and influences. This is the stage of pendulum theses and antitheses in the formation of her style. After the uncertainty, the critical struggle, comes the thankful stage where she finds herself, where she liberates herself from servility. Perceiving where her talents and her limitations lie, she can ascertain the level upon which she stands, and walk securely among her equals. Herein lies her originality, her integrity. Despite her experiments in modern forms, her writing becomes more similar in her succeeding books; the oscillation of the first two novels has passed. She does not obliterate influences; traces of the moderns, of Bergson, Proust, Joyce and T. S. Eliot are obvious. But now they are bent to serve her needs rather than to inhibit her through parasitic worship.

Although she classifies herself with the Georgian writers, the contemporaries of the reigning king, she is too deeply rooted in the romantic past to be called a strict Georgian. Her innovations are not revolutionary enough; she does not break with the past. She analyzes the Georgian rebellion against the literary convention: "Grammar is violated; syntax disintegrated" [42] yet she herself retains all the formulas. The Georgians, she feels, fall short because the "convention ceases to be a means of communication between writer and reader, and becomes an obstacle and an impediment." [43] Having determined for herself the weakness of contemporary literature, she seeks to evade its pitfalls by retaining the conventions of the past. She refuses to follow the herd blindly. She rejects the urge to be modern at any cost and take hand in "the smashing and the crashing . . . the prevailing sound of the Georgian age — rather a melancholy one if you think what melodious days there have been in the past, if you think of Shakespeare and Milton and Keats or even of Jane Austen and Thackeray and Dickens; if you think of the language, and the heights to which it can soar when free, and see the same eagle captive, bald, and croaking." [44]

Through her own classification of herself as well as through the evolution of her literary influences, she is seen as a transition writer, a bridge between the old and the new. English literary

---

[42] "Mr. Bennett and Mrs. Brown" p. 25.
[43] Ibid. p. 25.
[44] Ibid. p. 24.

style, the heritage of the classic poets and prose writers, is inherent in her word-groups, her imagery, her rhythm. And in her meditations and philosophy, she is the direct off-spring of the melancholy Englanders with their love of nature and their fear of death. She marks the end of a movement, the movement of rhythmic prose which, fresh in the hands of Sir Thomas Browne, reached its summit in the nineteenth century, in Ruskin and De Quincey. But where her dénouement, her culmination of the past, marks the foundation of her writing, she is still modern, sophisticatedly modern, intellectually modern. From the contemporary French Impressionists, she derives inspiration for the structure of her later novels; her speculations on time and space, are from the Bergsonian air she breathes. Yet though she abstracts phrases and casts and even trains of thought from the contemporaries, she never fully relinquishes her earlier influences. Supplemented by the moderns, the men of the classic past persist in molding her style.

And into this cleft between the past and present, she brings the unifying force of her feminine personality.

THE STYLE COMPLETED
AND THE THOUGHT IMPLIED

A variation of experiments, uninhibited by criticism and doubt, is ultimately liberated in Virginia Woolf, marking her completed style. Each of the succeeding novels represents a new nuance of innovation. Lyricism, feminine sensitivity, and a love of associations remain constant; the variable is the external structure which colors her lyricism but does not impede it. Denying masculine traditions as incompatible, she uses music as a vital medium in creating as a woman.

Music is the technical foundation for the short impressionistic life of a poetic romanticist, Jacob Flanders. As in orchestration, themes of life are played in "Jacob's Room", the theme of Jacob's life, his mother's life, the life of Clara, Sandra, Florinda, all the women he has loved. And blending them into harmony, is the great unifying theme of "Life" itself, the contemporary Georgian interest which replaced the "Nature" of the Romanticists and the medieval "God".

With contrapuntal technigue, sketches of the characters are given as they move in synchronic time. As though walking through a dance hall, Virginia Woolf notes down snatches of talk, which she uses in an experimental dialogue. New characters are introduced, revealed only through their fragmentary talk, while Clara, like the unifying theme in music, passes lightly in and out.

" 'Please', said Julia Eliot, taking up her position by the curtain almost opposite the door, 'don't introduce me. I like to look on. The amusing thing', she went on, addressing Mr. Salvin, who, owing to his lameness, was accommodated with a chair, 'the amusing thing about a party is to watch the people — coming and going, coming and going'.

'Last time we met', said Mr. Salvin, 'was at the Farquhars. Poor lady! She has much to put up with'.

'Doesn't she look charming?' exclaimed Miss Eliot, as Clara Durrant passed them.

'And which of them . . .?' asked Mr. Salvin, dropping his voice and speaking in quizzical tones.

'There are so many . . .' Miss Eliot replied. Three young men stood at the doorway looking about for their hostess.

'You don't remember Elizabeth as I do', said Mr. Salvin, 'dancing Highland reels at Banchorie. Clara lacks her mother's spirit. Clara is a little pale'.

'What different people one sees here!' said Miss Eliot.

'Happily we are not governed by the evening papers', said Mr. Salvin.

'I never read them', said Miss Eliot. 'I know nothing about politics', she added.

'The piano is in tune', said Clara, passing them, 'but we may have to ask some one to move it for us' ".[1]

Thus, like a music book of small completed themes, "Jacob's Room" is built upon little paragraphs, units in themselves, reflecting the mosaic perfection Virginia Woolf beholds in life. She sees not one law, not one great unified order, but small details, exquisite morceaux, which build in their correlation a unity of a different order: a feminine unity, a feminine aspect of life. The details, the paragraphs, stand at satisfactory rest in themselves, and in tone and context are harmoniously related to each other. With the technique of a musical rondeau, ending with the first strain repeated, the mood is induced. Sounded in the opening sentence, the theme is developed and varied until it reaches its climax, strangely deeper through the associations it has accumulated. In such meditated structure, Jacob's conflict between his love for a prostitute and his love for philosophic study, is described.

"The problem is insoluble. The body is harnessed to a brain. Beauty goes hand in hand with stupidity. There she sat staring at the fire as she had stared at the broken mustard-pot. In spite of defending indecency, Jacob doubted whether he liked it in the raw. He had a violent reversion towards male society, cloistered rooms, and the works of the classics; and was ready to turn with wrath upon whoever it was who had fashioned life thus.

"Then Florinda laid her hand upon his knee.

"After all, it was none of her fault. But the thought saddened him. It's not catastrophes, murders, deaths, diseases, that age and kill us; it's the way people look and laugh, and run up the steps of omnibuses.

"Any excuse, though serves a stupid woman. He told her his head ached.

"But when she looked at him, dumbly, half-guessing, half-understanding, apologising perhaps, anyhow saying as he had said, 'It's none of my fault', straight and beautiful in body, her face like a shell within its cap, then he knew that cloisters and classics are no use whatever. The problem is insoluble." [2]

Acknowledging her womanhood, Virginia Woolf is neither abstract in her philosophy of life, nor intellectual in her aesthetics. Life and style are her two main paths of interest. Like the early

---

[1] "Jacob's Room" p. 139.
[2] Ibid. p. 132.

poetic philosophers, like Jeremy Taylor and Sir Thomas Browne, she speculates, tormentedly, upon the riddle of the universe, conscious at times that questioning is useless. "At midnight . . . it would be foolish to vex the moor with questions — what? and why?" [3]

The emotional problems are inevitably expressed in surging rhythms. The phrases seem like the short lines of ballad verse, with deep caesuras. The writing is not intellectual, not philosophic, but ineffably poetic, emotionally feminine.

The delight in color and sound and smell, observed in "Orlando" and revealing Virginia Woolf's sensuous reaction to life, is now given unrestrained freedom. She plays with the senses: "a *breadth of water gleamed*" she writes with intentional aural confusion. The noise and musical movement in nature she describes with rhythmic onomatopœia:

"Up went the rooks and down again, rising in lesser numbers each time . . . The moss was soft; the tree-trunks spectral. Beyond them lay a silvery meadow. A breadth of water gleamed. Already the convolvulus moth was spinning over the flowers. Orange and purple, nasturtium and cherry pie, were washed into the twilight, but the tobacco plant and the passion flower, over which the great moth spun, were white as china. The rooks creaked their wings together on the tree-tops, and were settling down for sleep when, far off, a familiar sound shook and trembled — increased — fairly dinned in their ears — scared sleepy wings into the air again — the dinner bell at the house." [4] With curious artistry, she combines the human senses in one sentence, heavily weighted with suggestion. The sensation of sight is stimulated in "orange and purple", taste in "cherry pie", "were washed" (sound) "into the twilight" (time), "but the tobacco plant" (smell) "over which the great moth spun" (visual motion), "were white" (a repetition of the sight stimulus) "as china" (the sensation of touch).

Typical of the self-assurance with which she has now abandoned herself to imagery, she revels in phrases like "scared sleepy wings". She recalls Ruskin's polemics as well as his own use of pathetic fallacies. She repeats the confusion of vague imagery, of conceits which violate reality, which Ruskin had condemned but could not resist. In a quasi-philosophic meditation, she describes religion and morals in short associative flights. Night becomes an elongated sigh, and duty, a voice piping in a thread. "The Christians have the right to rouse most cities with their

---

[3] "Jacob's Room" p. 218.
[4] Ibid. p. 89.

interpretation of the day's meaning. Then, less melodiously, dissenters of different sects issue a cantankerous emendation . . . But nowadays it is the thin voice of duty, piping in a white thread from the top of a funnel, that collects the largest multitudes, and night is nothing but a long-drawn sigh between hammer-strokes, a deep breath — you can hear it from an open window even in the heart of London." [5]

The old ardent justification of admired writers, marked in "The Voyage Out" appears once more, but with mature confidence. Virginia Woolf now makes merry over adulation. Marlowe becomes the symbol of the worshipped past; "detest your own age," she burlesques Nick Greene.

"For example there is Mr. Masefield, there is Mr. Bennett. Stuff them into the flame of Marlowe and burn them to cinders. Let not a shred remain. Don't palter with the second rate. Detest your own age. Build a better one. . . . Useless to trust to the Victorians, who disembowel, or to the living, who are mere publicists." [6]

In the serene, detached presentation of her early struggle, her maturity is affirmed. Conflict is no longer a destructive force in her creations. Though her impulses lie essentially in one direction, she can without "protesting or preaching" appreciate the other. The conflict between rhapsody and restraint is objectified: "I like books whose virtue is all drawn together in a page or two. I like sentences that don't budge though armies cross them." (a repetition of the Gibbon's image and admiration in "The Voyage Out"). "I like words to be hard — such were Bonamy's views, and they won him the hostility of those whose taste is all for the fresh growths of the morning, who throw up the window, and find the poppies spread in the sun, and can't forbear a shout of jubilation at the astonishing fertility of English literature." [7]

Little is exposited in "Jacob's Room". Action, place, time and people are suggested impressionistically. There is a feminine delicacy of associations, a word, a repetition, which sets into motion the desired thoughts and more. The whole war is suggested in one line, almost obscured by its very simplicity. " 'The Kaiser', the far-away voice remarked in Whitehall, 'received me in audience.' " [8] And later, the war breaks out, but as a distant echo. One sees it through the half-closed eyes of a poetic woman.

---

[5] "Jacob's Room" p. 265.

[6] Ibid. p. 174.

[7] Ibid. p. 228.

[8] Ibid. p. 284.

" 'The guns?' said Betty Flanders, half asleep, getting out of bed and going to the window, which was decorated with a fringe of dark leaves.

"Not at this distance,' she thought. 'It is the sea.'

"Again, far away, she heard the dull sound, as if nocturnal women were beating great carpets. There was Morty lost, and Seabrook dead; her sons fighting for their country. But were the chickens safe? Was that some one moving downstairs? Rebecca with the toothache? No. The nocturnal women were beating great carpets. Her hens shifted slightly on their perches." [9]

It is the war behind the front; the war which women heard, but kept their chickens safe and fed more sons.

Jacob's death, sudden, unmotivated as are deaths in war, is only suggested by the desolation of his room, of his friend and his mother. It is the culmination; all of his existence is hurriedly recalled by his letters; in a description, repeated, of the room to which he had given life, his death in suggested with feminine artistry.

" 'He left everything just as it was,' Bonamy marvelled. 'Nothing arranged. All his letters strewn about for any one to read. What did he expect? Did he think he would come back?' he mused, standing in the middle of Jacob's room . . . .

"Bonamy took up a bill for a hunting-crop.

'That seems to be paid,' he said.

"There were Sandra's letters.

"Mrs. Durrant was taking a party to Greenwich.

"Lady Rocksbier hoped for the pleasure . . .

"Listless is the air in an empty room, just swelling the curtain; the flowers in the jar shift. One fibre in the wicker armchair creaks, though no one sits there." [10]

A wistful impression, this is more the living contrast than death itself.

The poetry "denied outlet" in women, now grows less and less constrained, and in "Mrs. Dalloway" knows little suppression. The Shelleyean relentless heaving of rhythmic verbs, "I die, I faint, I tremble, I expire"; the irresistible pressing forward to a culmination, is liberated here. The singing rhythms are inseparable from Virginia Woolf's emotional reaction to life. Her integrity asserts itself; the bald sobriety dictated by the critic is denied. Rhyme which has fallen largely out of poetry is introduced into prose, and her writing becomes more rhythmically poetic than much of contemporary verse.

---

[9] "Jacob's Room" p. 288.
[10] Ibid. p. 289; p. 61.

"So on a summer's day waves collect, over-balance, and fall; collect and fall; and the whole world seems to be saying 'that is all' more and more ponderously, until even the heart in the body which lies in the sun on the beach says too, That is all. Fear no more, says the heart. Fear no more, says the heart, committing its burden to some sea, which sighs collectively for all sorrows, and renews, begins, collects, lets fall. And the body alone listens to the passing bee; the wave breaking; the dog barking, far away barking and barking." [11]

Waves and heavings of the consciousness are, however fitting, not the only themes she now adapts to her lyric, feminine prose. Speeches are sung, characters speak in musical cadences. Not a dramatic monologue or a poetic play, but like an operetta, one word, one phrase, one rhythm is repeated: " 'But, thank you, Lucy, oh, thank you,' said Mrs. Dalloway, and thank you, thank you, she went on saying (sitting down on the sofa with her dress over her knees, her scissors, her silks), thank you, thank you, she went on saying in gratitude . . . ." [12] The lyrical fluidity suggests the sweep and graceful movement of the operatic stage.

Dialogue, however, is not abundant; realism, the sharp selectivity, demanded by a dramatist, is lacking. Virginia Woolf is lyrical, singing and receiving vague irrational impressions. " 'She was like a lily, Sally said, a lily by the side of a pool' ".[13] Or "She was like a poplar, she was like a river, she was like a hyacinth, Willie Titcomb was thinking." [14] It is like the richly colored, dreamy conversation of "Salome", a soliloquy of the consciousness, thought more than spoken. In silence, Peter Walsh remembers how he had wanted to marry Clarissa Dalloway, and in silence, she understands his thoughts.

"Of course I did, thought Peter;" in his desire to marry Clarissa; "it almost broke my heart too, he thought; and was overcome with his own grief, which rose like a moon looked at from a terrace, ghastly beautiful with light from the sunken day. I was more unhappy than I've ever been since, he thought. And as if in truth he were sitting there on the terrace he edged a little towards Clarissa; put his hand out; raised it; let it fall." [15]

The poetic swelling of emotions, the rhythmic surging of associations in the human mind, is artfully suggested by the style. With unusual structure, prose flows into poetry and long waves

---

[11] "Mrs. Dalloway" p. 55.
[12] Ibid. p. 54.
[13] Ibid. p. 268.
[14] Ibid. p. 262.
[15] Ibid. p. 58.

of thoughts and illusions are set into graceful motion. "A sound interrupted him; a frail   quivering sound, a voice bubbling up without direction, vigour, beginning or end, running weakly and shrilly and with an absence of all human meaning into

       ee um fah um so

       foo swee too eem oo —

the voice of no age or sex, the voice of an ancient spring spouting from the earth; which issued, just opposite Regent's Park Tube Station, from a tall quivering shape, like a funnel, like a rusty pump, like a wind-beaten tree for ever barren of leaves which lets the wind run up and down its branches singing

       ee um fah um so

       foo swee too eem oo,

and rocks and creaks and moans in the eternal breeze." [16]

In turning to the world of the sub-conscious, Virginia Woolf finds fitting cause for hallucinations. The associative conceits of nature, loved by the romanticists and condemned by their critics, are permissible in the consciousness, and Mrs. Dalloway, feeling that another woman is crushing her, believes she can "hear twigs cracking and feel hooves planted down in the depths of that leaf-encumbered forest, the soul." [17] The darkness of this underworld allows a vagueness of images which sunlight repels. Where earlier writers fell back upon dreams to absolve many impossible illusions, Virginia Woolf, like the psycho-analytic novelists, seeks out this dream world consciously. There "are the visions which ceaselessly float up, pace beside, put their faces in front of, the actual thing." [18] She still perceives the duality between fact and fancy, but in the dream-world, illusions become reality, justifying a haziness and extravagance otherwise absurd. "Such are the visions which proffer great cornucopias full of fruit to the solitary traveller, or murmur in his ear like sirens lolloping away on the green sea waves, or are dashed in his face like bunches of roses, or rise to the surface like pale faces which fishermen flounder through floods to embrace." [19] Heaped together, unobjectified, the very conceits satirized in "Orlando" are now allowed because they make no pretence at reality. They exist in trauma and there they are absolute. It is the indelible mark of her character, that, needing expression for such poetic fancies, Virginia Woolf seeks a form in which they are acceptable. Dreams are a refuge, a precaution. At all costs, poetry must find outlet.

[16] "Mrs. Dalloway" p. 112.
[17] Ibid. p. 17.
[18] Ibid. p. 79.
[19] Ibid. p. 79.

The tradition that women think emotionally is embodied in Clarissa Dalloway. Her thoughts are a firework of ejaculations; of poetic visions and feminine ecstasy. " 'What a lark!' 'What a plunge!' " she cries typically in the first page, her introduction: "How fresh, how calm, stiller than this of course, the air was in the early morning; like the flap of a wave; the kiss of a wave; chill and sharp and yet (for a girl of eighteen as she then was) solemn, feeling as she did, standing there at the open window, that something awful was about to happen; looking at the flowers, at the trees with the smoke winding off them and the rooks rising, falling; standing and looking until Peter Walsh said, 'Musing among the vegetables?' — was that it? — 'I prefer men to cauli-flowers' — was that it?" [20]

The logical procession of ideas, attributed to men, is foreign to Clarissa. She has flashes of intuition, of reminiscences, whose strong emotional appeal compels cadences and imagery. Lest she lose the common touch with prose, Virginia Woolf intercepts the phrases that threaten to grow metrical, with parenthetic prosaic remarks. Yet the rhythmic, bubbling talk is as typical of Virginia Woolf as it is of Mrs. Dalloway. She is a compound writer rather than a complex one; her thoughts are ordered in *ands* and *buts*. Her sentences are clever windings and turnings of gushing irrelevancies. The long lists observed in "Orlando" and rever-berating here would prove the adage that women cannot select; all their observations must be aired.

"For it was the middle of June. The War was over . . . The King and Queen were at the Palace. And everywhere, though it was still so early, there was a beating, a stirring of galloping ponies, tapping of cricket-bats; Lords, Ascot, Ranelagh and all the rest of it; wrapped in the soft mesh of the grey-blue morning air, which, as the day wore on, would unwind them, and set down on their lawns and pitches the bouncing ponies, whose forefeet just struck the ground and up they sprung, the whirling young men, and laughing girls in their transparent muslins who, even now, after dancing all night, were taking their absurd woolly dogs for a run; and even now, at this hour, discreet old dowagers were shooting out in their motor cars on errands of mystery; and the shopkeepers were fidgeting in their windows with their paste and diamonds, their lovely old sea-green brooches in eighteenth-century settings to tempt Americans (but one must economise, not buy things rashly for Elizabeth), and she, too, loving it as she did with an absurd and faithful passion, being part of it, since her people were courtiers once in the time of the Georges, she, too,

---

[20] Ibid. p. 5.

was going that very night to kindle and illuminate; to give her party. But how strange, on entering the Park, the silence; the mist; the hum; the slow-swimming happy ducks; the pouched birds waddling . . ." [21]

The thoughts run on like a gossippy woman; the long full sentence is less a structural feat than a psychologic one, giving the hurrying, bustling tokens of the hurrying, bustling observations and ideas. It is such writing which makes "Mrs. Dalloway" the unquestionable product of a woman. In it Virginia Woolf has found free scope to explore the consciousness of her sex. Mrs. Dalloway is representative of the emotional, quasi-poetic woman whose thoughts are largely memories. She is "the perfect hostess", the social analogy of the great Mother, "with that extraordinary gift, that woman's gift of making a world of her own wherever she happened to be." [22] Her irrelevancies are traces, depicting the mysterious leaps in the mind of a woman from vanity to the most profound experiences in life and back again to the question of dresses and personal beauty.

"That was her self —", she thinks, looking in the mirror, "pointed; dartlike; definite. That was her self when some effort, some call on her to be her self, drew the parts together." (Orlando too as a woman, draws her parts together, the innumerable phases and potentialities which make her "true self . . . compact of all the selves we have it in us to be; commanded and locked up by the Captain self, the Key self, which amalgamates and controls them all"). So with the same mosaic quality of a woman's personality, Mrs. Dalloway "drew the parts together, she alone knew how different, how incompatible and composed so for the world only into one centre, one diamond, one woman who sat in her drawing-room and made a meeting-point, a radiancy no doubt in some dull lives, a refuge for the lonely to come to, perhaps; she had helped young people, who were grateful to her; had tried to be the same always, never showing a sign of all the other sides of her — faults, jealousies, vanities, suspicions, like this of Lady Bruton not asking her to lunch; which, she thought (combing her hair finally), is utterly base! Now, where was her dress?" [23]

Streams of consciousness are explored in all the characters. The present is a kind of maypole from which each character flees with his own streamer back into the past. The characters reminisce; their lives are recounted with a constant moving backward in time. Nothing is active and vital; the figures are forever contemplating, always regretting, or longing sentimentally for

[21] Ibid. p. 7.
[22] "Orlando" p. 262.
[23] "Mrs. Dalloway" p. 52.

times past. "There was Regent's Park — odd, he thought, how the thought of childhood keeps coming back to me — the result of seeing Clarissa, perhaps; for women live much more in the past than we do, he thought. They attach themselves to places; and their fathers — a woman's always proud of her father." [24]

All feminine irrelevancies are unified in this stream of consciousness; associations, as of Clarissa's father, stimulate in Virginia Woolf, aphorisms which mark her life as one rich in observations and experience. Peter's reflection that women live deeply in the past is a justification of the whole book, a justification of Clarissa's constant reminiscences and, more important, of Virginia Woolf's own mentality, inducing her to create in such scant action and vast, poetic memories, as:

"Still remembering how once in some primeval May she had walked with her lover, this rusty pump, this battered old woman with one hand exposed for coppers, the other clutching her side, would still be there in ten million years, remembering how once she had walked in May, where the sea flows now, with whom it did not matter — he was a man, oh yes, a man who had loved her. But the passage of ages had blurred the clarity of that ancient May day; the bright petalled flowers were hoar and silver frosted; and she no longer saw, when she implored him (as she did now quite clearly) 'look in my eyes with thy sweet eyes intently,' she no longer saw brown eyes, black whiskers or sunburnt face, but only a looming shape, a shadow shape . . ." [25]

Where in "Jacob's Room" the method is contrapuntal, in "Mrs. Dalloway" it is a constant retracing of past themes. The sharp outlines of the present are blurred; here is a dreaming of the past, of associations which have lost their temporal significance. There is little of the active movement of the first two novels; the characters contemplate a move and then regard its completion. The action itself is rarely mentioned; its reality lies in its suggestiveness that space and time have been traversed. A character thinks of holding something; no action occurs, but the object is obtained and held. "But he wanted to come in holding something. Flowers? Yes, flowers, since he did not trust his taste in gold; any number of flowers, roses, orchids, to celebrate what was, reckoning things as you will, an event; this feeling about her when they spoke of Peter Walsh at luncheon; and they never spoke of it; not for years had they spoken of it; which, he thought, grasping his red and white roses together (a vast bunch in tissue paper), is the greatest mistake in the world." [26]

[24] "Mrs. Dalloway" p. 77.
[25] Ibid. p. 114.
[26] Ibid. p. 159.

Where in her earlier novels, she had returned to Sir Thomas Browne and the dead philosophers for inspiration, she stands now in the air of her time. It is Bergson's problem and solutions which modulate her thinking and with it her style. The poetic concept of reality, peculiar to the French philosopher, is the kernel of her writing. She is too innately creative, too inherently Bergsonian to be called Bergson's imitator. It is conceivable that she would have found the way without him; yet living in the Bergsonian atmosphere, she draws even unconsciously from the truths he had established. Life is to be understood, he had proclaimed, not through the brain or mechanical reason, but through poetic intuition. A manifesto for Virginia Woolf to whom as poet and woman, intuition is core and kernel. Like Bergson, she denounces science in its attempt to explain mechanically the processes of the mind and the human consciousness. She objectifies her distaste for science in the doctors she creates. Portraying Science in one man, Dr. Bradshaw, she ridicules its complacent external logic, and its utter failure to understand the deeper psychic experiences in man. Only intuition, sympathetic and creative, can grasp these inner phenomena. Mrs. Dalloway, in her Bergsonian irrationalism, can comprehend the torments which drive Septimus Warren Smith to insanity; Dr. Bradshaw can only diagnose with "his infallible instinct, this is madness, this sense." [27] He can codify insanities; he cannot comprehend them. To all his patients he gives the same rational cure, regardless of what has caused their psychosis or how fitting to each of them his cure may be. With driving irony, Virginia Woolf portrays this man of reason, his logical orderly classifications and his role of fatal critic to the Bergsonian creative poet. "To his patients he gave three-quarters of an hour; and if in this exacting science which has to do with what, after all, we know nothing about — the nervous system, the human brain — a doctor loses his sense of proportion, as a doctor he fails. Health we must have; and health is proportion; so that when a man comes into your room and says he is Christ (a common delusion), and has a message, as they mostly have, and threatens, as they often do, to kill himself, you invoke proportion; order rest in bed; rest in solitude; silence and rest; rest without friends, without books, without messages; six month's rest; until a man who went in weighing seven stone six comes out weighing twelve." [28]

The scientist, in his mechanical ratiocination, has missed the central difficulty; he can cure the body, but for psychic diseases, his masculine brain alone is impotent. It is the unscien-

[27] Ibid. p. 138.
[28] Ibid. p. 137.

tific Clarissa who penetrates with peculiar femininity, why, after Septimus has visited Dr. Bradshaw, he commits suicide.. "there were the poets and thinkers. Suppose he had had that passion, and had gone to Sir William Bradshaw, a great doctor, yet to her obscurely evil, without sex or lust, extremely polite to women, but capable of some indescribable outrage — forcing your soul, that was it — if this young man had gone to him, and Sir William had impressed him, like that, with his power, might he not then have said (indeed she felt it now), Life is made intolerable; they make life intolerable, men like that?" [29] Or, she philosophizes: "A thing there was that mattered; a thing, wreathed about with chatter, defaced, obscured in her own life, let drop every day in corruption, lies, chatter. This he had preserved. Death was defiance. Death was an attempt to communicate, people feeling the impossibility of reaching the center which, mystically, evaded them; closeness drew apart; rapture faded, one was alone. There was an embrace in death.

"But this young man who had killed himself — had he plunged holding his treasure?" [30]

The change in Virginia Woolf's philosophic influences is obvious in her style. Her nature descriptions do not change, but her analysis of the consciousness, her psychic interest in life, seeks a fitting expression. From the poetic rhythms of Browne and Lamb and De Quincey, whose cadences, in their harmonic purity, seem to follow laws of aural rhetoric, she now assumes the Bergsonian rhythms which convey the rise and fall of thoughts themselves. Her old search for the Flaubert *mot juste,* seems suppressed. Single words are not ostentatiously sounded but are blended to depict the sensitive workings of the mind. She is following carefully Bergson's definition of style. «En réalité, l'art de l'écrivain consiste surtout à nous faire oublier qu'il emploie des mots . . . Le rhythme de la parole n'a donc d'autre objet que de reproduire le rhythme de la pensée.» [31]

Bergson's vitalism, his creative Élan Vital, and his definition of style mark their influence upon Virginia Woolf. His differentiation between measured time and the creative time-concept of the consciousness stimulate in her a deep train of thought. "Time . . . though it makes animals and vegetables bloom and fade with amazing punctuality, has no such simple effect upon the mind of man. The mind of man, moreover, works with equal strangeness upon the body of time. An hour, once it lodges in the queer element of the human spirit, may be stretched to fifty or a

---

[29] "Mrs. Dalloway" p. 257.
[30] Ibid. p. 256.
[31] "L'Ame et le Corps" p. 44.

hundred times its clock length; on the other hand, an hour may be accurately represented on the timepiece of the mind by one second. This extraordinary discrepancy between time on the clock and time in the mind is less known than it should be and deserves fuller investigation." [32]

Bergson's durée, parallel to the inner stream of consciousness, is for Virginia Woolf, the irrational dynamic reality in life. Consciousness, Bergson contended, is comprehended largely in temporal impressions. The man of action, observes Virginia Woolf, is different from the sedentary thinker in his apprehension of passing time: "time when he is thinking becomes inordinately long; time when he is doing becomes inordinately short . . . his whole past, which seemed to him of extreme length and variety, rushed into the falling second, swelled it a dozen times its natural size, coloured it a thousand tints, and filled it with all the odds and ends in the universe." [33]

It is in this psychic creative memory, where the measured laws of time and space are shattered, that Virginia Woolf approximates Bergson's Élan Vital. She builds the characters in "Mrs. Dalloway" through their own recreation of time past, a Bergsonian influence upon Proust and Joyce and through them upon contemporary literature.

Following the technique of "Ulysses", "Mrs. Dalloway" revives the Aristotelian unities of time, place and action. The single ordinary day depicted in both novels is the middle of June where the characters may bathe, like Stephen, in the morning, or sleep on benches at noon, like Peter Walsh. London in "Mrs. Dalloway" supersedes Joyce's Dublin with the same place-consciousness. Westminster, Bond Street, Regent's Park, are vital, conscious settings as suggestive of defined space as Davy Byrne's bar, or Eccles Street, or the Lying-in-Hospital in Dublin. The characters are held together in "Mrs. Dalloway" with more obvious, more conscious unity and rigour than in "Ulysses". Where Joyce's characters drift and fall apart as in the course of an ordinary day, and Bloom and Stephen are driven together only by the subconscious Odyssean search of a father for a son, Virginia Woolf's characters are gravitated through external motivations. Clarissa's party is the great cohesive goal towards which they all converge. Through secondary streams, the whole world seems connected; shopkeepers, florists, department stores, omnibuses, everything touched by the characters becomes centripetal. "It was her street, this, Clarissa's; cabs were rushing round the corner,

---

[32] "Orlando" p. 83.
[33] Ibid. p. 83.

like water round the piers of a bridge, drawn together, it seemed to him because they bore people going to her party, Clarissa's party."[34] Septimus, a vital character for Virginia Woolf, a poet shocked by the war, whose wild fanciful illusions have grown unrestrained with the loss of his stability, seems unrelated to the others, neither going to the party nor known to Clarissa. Until the end, he seems to have been inserted only for the potentialities he has, excusable in a deranged man, for poetic flight. But at the party itself, the thread which relates him to the others becomes apparent. It is through his doctor, the successful Harley Street specialist, who attends the party, that Septimus is a necessary tributary stream.

Where the party is the goal of adherence, Big Ben is the ineluctable clasp between the characters, the great unity, symbol of time, of the present. It strikes inexorably. Each one hears it, in a different place, in a different mood, in a different action, yet for that one second all are linked consciously together.

"Big Ben struck the half-hour.

"How extraordinary it was, strange, yes touching to see the old lady (they had been neighbours ever so many years) move away from the window, as if she were attached to that sound, that string. Gigantic as it was, it had something to do with her. Down, down, into the midst of ordinary things the finger fell making the moment solemn. She was forced, so Clarissa imagined, by that sound, to move, to go — but where? . . .

"Volubly, troublously, the late clock sounded, coming in on the wake of Big Ben, with its lap full of trifles. Beaten up, broken up by the assault of carriages, the brutality of vans, the eager advance of myriads of angular men, of flaunting women, the domes and spires of offices and hospitals, the last relics of this lap full of odds and ends seemed to break, like the spray of an exhausted wave, upon the body of Miss Kilman standing still in the street for a moment to mutter 'It is the flesh'."[35]

The fifteen minutes between a quarter of twelve and noon consume fifty pages of elucidation, of tracing the mental reversions to the past. As in Proust, the interest in time evinces a peculiar philosophic trend in Virginia Woolf's mentality; it is her problem of mortality. Between the flowing cycles of life and death, time is irrevocable. "The clock began striking. The young man had killed himself; but she did not pity him; with the clock striking the hour, one, two, three, she did not pity him; with all this going on . . . She felt somehow very like him — the young man

---

[34] "Mrs. Dalloway" p. 228.
[35] Ibid. p. 176.

who had killed himself. She felt glad that he had done it; thrown it away while they went on living. The clock was striking. The leaden circles dissolved in the air. But she must go back. She must assemble. She must find Sally and Peter. And she came in from the little room." [36]

To her feminine perception, the philosophic enigma of time offers another stimulus of poetic beauty. Time is an experience more than a concept. She describes it not as a dialectic thinker but as a poet, sensitive to its lyrical associations. The simple stimulus " 'It is time' " given by Septimus' Italian wife, evokes fanciful reactions which play with the word as well as its concept. "The word 'time' split its husk; poured its riches over him; and from his lips fell like shells, like shavings from a plane, without his making them, hard, white, imperishable, words, and flew to attach themselves to their places in an ode to Time; an immortal ode to Time." [37]

This feminine impressionism, content to experience time simply as a sensation, is deepened in "Orlando" where time becomes a philosophic experiment. The hypothesis of one life developing through three centuries shows a new phase in Virginia Woolf's temporal concern; a cerebral rather than sensory excitement. A subtle reversion has occurred in her picture of the march of time; in "Jacob's Room" it is the inevitable succession of one day, one measured interval by another; it is the normal ascendency in time which had characterized the first two novels. In "Orlando" the normal is variated; Orlando moves forward with the same inevitability with which Jacob matures, but at a different tempo. An arbitrary ratio of one year to civilization's ten might be erected; Orlando lives through a time succession of more than three hundred years, growing approximately thirty years old. This fitful redisposition of time is not only a romantic conjecture but is founded upon the maxims of philosophy. Einstein, disproving an absolute time-concept and making relativity of time absolute, demonstrated that since two lightrays can move at a different speed in relation to each other, so two men can move at a relatively different tempo in space. Thus it is conceivable that while one man may move very rapidly and reach an age of eighty sun years, another may remain in inertia with eternal youth, or move relatively slower. While the measured calendar time progresses from Shakespeare to the present and more than fifteen generations of men live and die, Orlando progresses in a time peculiar to himself through the same

---

[36] "Mrs. Dalloway" p. 259.
[37] Ibid. p. 97.

space. It is a poetization of Einstein's hypothesis: „Nicht der Raumpunkt, in dem etwas geschieht, nicht der Zeitpunkt, in dem etwas geschieht, hat physikalische Realität, sondern nur das Ereignis selbst. Zwischen zwei Ereignissen gibt es keine absolute (vom Bezugsraum unabhängige) räumliche und keine absolute zeitliche Beziehung, wohl aber eine absolute (von der Wahl des Bezugsraumes unabhängige) zeiträumliche Beziehung." [38] Orlando is a physical possibility in a time-space continuum. Ignorant of the relative speed in which the average man matures, he is naturally unconscious that his motion is retarded. Apprehending only his own time-progress, he perceives no discrepancy in knowing Queen Elizabeth, as a child, Pope and Johnson at thirty, and Victoria and the contemporaries only a few years later.

The possibilites which such a dislocation of time offer to imaginative literature have been acknowledged before, with most acclaim perhaps in Mark Twain's "A Connecticut Yankee in King Arthur's Court". John Lloyd Balderston's drama, "Berkeley Square" appearing in the same year as "Orlando", employs a plot also founded in relativity. A man of the twentieth century returns to the eighteenth, like a refracted or retarded lightray. By retracing two hundred years of space, he possesses knowledge of the completed actions and spoken words existing permanently in space. He can predict with surety all that the characters are yet to do. The future for them is a completed past in his experience. Like "Orlando" and "A Connecticut Yankee", "Berkeley Square" is a fantasy; the play of time lends itself to humor. In Virginia Woolf's personality, laughter is a vital element.

But tragedy and hopelessness are implicit also in her scrutiny of time. Despite creative mental variations, there are cycles of seasons and years and, more sorrowfully, of deaths. All striving, all individual ambitions and creations seem as nothing in the face of eternity, when "the very stone one kicks with one's boot will outlast Shakespeare." [39] The law of the universe builds the vast background of "To the Lighthouse". The uncontrollable procession of ages of time, broods over the two living days described. The Bergsonian problems of personal and physical time have been swept into the boundless problems of infinity. The past and present, all-important before, now lose their meaning, as Virginia Woolf grows more conscious of their ultimate fate.

The timeless cycles of life and death, speculations of the earliest religions, lie at the basis of all her thought. It is not

---

[38] "Relativitätstheorie" p. 20.
[39] "To the Lighthouse" p. 59.

the immediate problem of "to be or not to be", but a remoter
enigma of how long to be — of eternal existence or transitory
fame. The present is vital, is not to be annihilated; it is the
foundation upon which personal immortality must rest. But
tragedy is deep-rooted wherever the will for fame is greater than
the power. Mr. Ramsay, the scholarly professor, is tragically
aware of his limitations, of his puny temporal fame. Yet in the
face of futility, Virginia Woolf makes him persevere, obstinately,
admirably. In a dramatic struggle, he "consecrated his effort to
arrive at a perfectly clear understanding of the problem which
now engaged the energies of his splendid mind.

"It was a splendid mind. For if thought is like the keyboard
of a piano, divided into so many notes, or like the alphabet is
ranged in twenty-six letters all in order, then his splendid mind
had no sort of difficulty in running over those letters one by
one, firmly and accurately, until it had reached, say, the letter Q.
He reached Q. Very few people in the whole of England ever
reach Q. Here, stopping for one moment by the stone urn which
held the geraniums, he saw, but now far far away, like children
picking up shells, divinely innocent and occupied with little trifles
at their feet and somehow defenceless against a doom which he
perceived, his wife and son, together, in the window. They needed
his protection; he gave it them. But after Q? What comes next?
After Q there are a number of letters the last of which is scarcely
visible to mortal eyes, but glimmers red in the distance. Z is only
reached once by one man in a generation. Still if he could reach
R it would be something. Here at least was Q. He dug his heels
in at Q. Q he was sure of. Q he could demonstrate. If Q then
is Q — R — Here he knocked his pipe out, with two or three
resonant taps on the ram's horn which made the handle of the
urn, and proceeded. 'Then R . . .' He braced himself. He
clenched himself.

"Qualities that would have saved a ship's company exposed
on a broiling sea with six biscuits and a flask of water — endurance
and justice, foresight, devotion, skill, came to his help. R is then
— what is R?" [40]

Genius? Who is a genius — the riddle Virginia Woolf
delves into her own mind to fathom, is significantly threshed
out by Mr. Ramsay, who "could see, without wishing it, that old,
that obvious distinction between the two classes of men; on the
one hand the steady goers of superhuman strength who, plodding
and persevering, repeat the whole alphabet in order, twenty-six
letters in all, from start to finish; on the other the gifted, the

---

[40] "To the Lighthouse" p. 56.

inspired who, miraculously, lump all the letters together in one flash — the way of genius. He had not genius; he laid no claim to that: but he had, or might have had, the power to repeat every letter of the alphabet from A to Z accurately in order. Meanwhile, he stuck at Q. On, then, on to R . . .

"Yet he would not die lying down; he would find some crag of rock, and there, his eyes fixed on the storm, trying to the end to pierce the darkness, he would die standing. He would never reach R." [41] The victim of time and mortality.

Where "Jacob's Room" was built upon a normal succession of recorded days, and "Mrs. Dalloway" upon a static unit, one day through which the past became dynamic, "To the Lighthouse" is a synthesis of both. The one day is expanded to two, suggesting an interim in the common course of time. The children of the first day are grown in the second, many have married, the war has been fought, many are dead. The two days described appear as the summits of two ocean waves, bound together by the fall and reascent of time. With stylistic adaptation, the flowingness of time is echoed in the writing. The darkness of night is symbolic of this interim where all shapes appear in their primal amorphousness. Sleep is synonymous with death; the accidents of living form are shrouded.

"So with the lamps all put out, the moon sunk, and a thin rain drumming on the roof a down-pouring of immense darkness began. Nothing, it seemed, could survive the flood, the profusion of darkness which, creeping in at keyholes and crevices, stole round window blinds, came into bedrooms, swallowed up here a jug and basin, there a bowl of red and yellow dahlias, there the sharp edges and firm bulk of a chest of drawers. Not only was furniture confounded; there was scarcely anything left of body or mind by which one could say 'This is he' or 'This is she'. Sometimes a hand was raised as if to clutch something or ward off something, or somebody groaned, or somebody laughed aloud as if sharing a joke with nothingness." [42]

In the wider voids of space, of "nothingness", time loses its significance. There is a poetic fatalism, and yet Virginia Woolf does not lose her active interest in life. Decay is inevitable, but only through new life is it apprehensible. In the interlude between the two days, she depicts the mortality in time, yet it is "certain airs", vestiges of life, which repudiate a complete non-being. "Nothing stirred in the drawing-room or in the dining-room or on the staircase. Only through the rusty hinges and

[41] Ibid. p. 58.
[42] "To the Lighthouse" p. 195.

swollen sea-moistened wood-work certain airs, detached from the body of the wind (the house was ramshackle after all) crept round corners and ventured indoors. Almost one might imagine them, as they entered the drawing-room, questioning and wondering, toying with the flap of hanging wall-paper, asking, would it hang much longer, when would it fall? Then smoothly brushing the walls, they passed on musingly as if asking the red and yellow roses on the wall-paper whether they would fade, and questioning (gently, for there was time at their disposal) the torn letters in the wastepaper basket, the flowers, the books, all of which were now open to them and asking. Were they allies? Were they enemies? How long would they endure?

"So some random light directing them from an uncovered star, or wandering ship, or the Lighthouse even, with its pale footfall upon stair and mat, the little airs mounted the staircase and nosed round bedroom doors. But here surely, they must cease. Whatever else may perish and disappear what lies here is steadfast. Here one might say to those sliding lights, those fumbling airs, that breathe and bend over the bed itself, here you can neither touch nor destroy." [43] The bed is, with curious mysticism, protected from decay. It is the symbol of organic life.

This is no pessimism, "no literature of negation to the point of being nihilist", [44] wich Harold Nicolson describes as typical of Virginia Woolf. Some flash of hope appears within the deepest chaos, the most desperate doubt. Futility is a passing attitude; it only "seems impossible" from the wrecks of physical and inner storms, to compose once more "a perfect whole or read in the littered pieces the clear words of truth. For our penitance deserves a glimpse only; our toil respite only." [45] Even where a philosophy of futilitarianism seems most compelling, traces of residual hope appear. *"Almost it would appear* that it is useless in such confusion to ask the night those questions as to what, and why, and wherefore, which tempt the sleeper from his bed to seek an answer." [46] A shattering hopeless nihilism would not modify itself with "almost" and "it would appear". Virginia Woolf's nocturnal questioning of the universe, loses its pessimistic despair in the coming of day. "Now, day after day, light turned, like a flower reflected in water, its clear image on the wall opposite . . . Loveliness and stillness clasped hands in the bedroom, and among the shrouded jugs and sheeted chairs even the prying of the wind, and the soft nose of the clammy sea airs,

---

[43] "To the Lighthouse" p. 196.
[44] "The New Spirit in Literature" p. 23,
[45] "To the Lighthouse" p. 199.
[46] Ibid. p. 199.

rubbing, snuffling, iterating, and reiterating their questions — 'Will you fade? Will you perish?' — scarcely disturbed the peace, the indifference, the air of pure integrity, as if the question they asked scarcely needed that they should answer: we remain." [47]

This is the flaunt in the face of futility: "we remain". There is no still-standing, life moves in Heraclitean waves of ebb and flow. There are moments when the house seems on the verge of destruction, when, as the toll of time, disintegration seems the only certainty. "The house was left; the house was deserted. It was left like a shell on a sandhill to fill with dry salt grains now that life had left it. The long night seemed to have set in . . ." [48] But the forces of life are unceasingly at play.

"For now had come that moment, that hesitation when dawn trembles and night pauses, when if a feather alight in the scale it will be weighed down. One feather, and the house, sinking, falling, *would have* turned and pitched downwards to the depths of darkness. In the ruined room, picnickers would have lit their kettles; lovers sought shelter there, lying on the bare boards; and the shepherd stored his dinner on the bricks, and the tramp slept with his coat round him to ward off the cold. Then the roof would have fallen; briars and hemlocks would have blotted out path, step, and window; would have grown, unequally but lustily over the mound, until some trespasser, losing his way, could have told only by a red-hot poker among the nettles, or a scrap of china in the hemlock, that here once some one had lived; there had been a house.

"If the feather had fallen, if it had tipped the scale downwards, the whole house would have plunged to the depths to lie upon the sands of oblivion." [49] But the supposition is too morose, too nihilistic. The wave of existence must rise again. Everywhere Virginia Woolf perceives some hint of life, even if only the potential life residual in decay. "But there was a force working; something not highly conscious; something that leered, something that lurched; something not inspired to go about its work with dignified ritual or solemn chanting. Mrs. McNab groaned; Mrs. Bast creaked. They were old; they were stiff; their legs ached . . . Slowly and painfully, with broom and pail, mopping, scouring, Mrs. McNab, Mrs. Bast stayed the corruption and the rot; rescued from the pool of time that was fast closing over them now a basin, now a cupboard; . . ." [50]

[47] "To the Lighthouse" p. 200.
[48] Ibid. p. 212.
[49] Ibid. p. 214.
[50] Ibid. p. 215.

The dark shapelessness has been penetrated, and once more from the chaos, there is light. "The pool of Time" is symbolic of the whole philosophy of the novel, of Virginia Woolf's return from the immediate subjective problems of Bergson and Joyce to the more fundamental meditations of Sir Thomas Browne. The writing encloses these thoughts of potential life like a swelling placenta. "Nothing it seemed could break that image, corrupt that innocence, or disturb the swaying mantle of silence which, week after week, in the empty room, wove into itself the falling cries of birds, ships hooting, the drone and hum of the fields, a dog's bark, a man's shout, and folded them round the house in silence." [51]

Poetic rhythms become more than, as in "The Voyage Out", the expression of subjective emotions, or of streaming thoughts as in "Mrs. Dalloway". Like stage direktions, they now convey the action: "As she lurched (for she rolled like a ship at sea) and leered (for her eyes fell on nothing directly, but with a sidelong glance that deprecated the scorn and anger of the world — she was witless, she knew it), as she clutched the banisters and hauled herself upstairs and rolled from room to room, she sang." [52] The form is the manifest clue to the content; the washerwoman, cleaning the house after its long decay, is described with the childlike rhythms of a popular ballad. All her simple mentality, all her consciousness, all her philosophy is implicit in the weary, sing-song rhythms, "how it was one long sorrow and trouble, how it was getting up and going to bed again, and bringing things out and putting them away again." [53] And yet, even to this common woman of the folk, to whom life is a monotonous pendulum of living and dying, there are moments of hope which make nihilism impossible. She has known sorrow, yet the memory of a joy somewhere, bars her as it bars Virginia Woolf, from pessimism.

"It was not easy or snug this world she had known for close on seventy years. Bowed down she was with weariness. How long, she asked, creaking and groaning on her knees under the bed, dusting the boards, how long shall it endure? but hobbled to her feet again, pulled herself up, and again with her sidelong leer which slipped and turned aside even from her own face, and her own sorrows, stood and gaped in the glass, aimlessly smiling, and began again the old amble and hobble, taking up mats, putting down china, looking sidewards in the glass, as if,

[51] "To the Lighthouse" p. 201.
[52] Ibid. p. 202.
[53] Ibid. p. 203.

after all, she had her consolations, as if indeed there twined about her dirge some incorrigible hope. Visions of joy there must have been at the wash-tub, say with her children (yet two had been base-born and one had deserted her), at the public-house, drinking; turning over scraps in her drawers. Some cleavage of the dark there must have been, some channel in the depths of obscurity through which light enough issued to twist her face grinning in the glass and make her, turning to her job again, mumble out the old music hall song. Meanwhile the mystic, the visionary, walked the beach, stirred a puddle, looked at a stone, and asked themselves 'What am I?' 'What is this' and suddenly an answer was vouchsafed them (what it was they could not say): so that they were warm in the frost and had comfort in the desert. But Mrs. McNab continued to drink and gossip as before." [54]

The structural counterpoint is closely reminiscent of "Jacob's Room". Many of the stylistic tricks of the earlier novel are repeated here, at times more pronounced, at others, suggested lightly, as though too fully consumed to need duplication. The conceit of showing death through the room which Jacob had charged with life, is here expanded to the house in which the Ramsays and their friends had moved. And progressing one step farther, Virginia Woolf shows the house after its decomposition, again inhabited with life.

She repeats the musical compositions, which in "Jacob's Room" she had made of her paragraphs: closed structural units, ushered in and resolved by the same chord.

"Never did anybody look so sad. Bitter and black, half-way down, in the darkness, in the shaft which ran from the sunlight to the depths, perhaps a tear formed; a tear fell; the waters swayed this way and that, received it, and were at rest. Never did anybody look so sad." [55]

The music, suggested in this structure, is later augmented, and from a Schubert melody becomes tumultuous, combining the Wagnerian elements of poetry and sound and action. "He shivered; he quivered. All his vanity, all his satisfaction in his own splendour, riding fell as a thunderbolt, fierce as a hawk at the head of his men through the valley of death, had been shattered, destroyed. Stormed at by shot and shell, boldly we rode and well, flashed through the valley of death, volleyed and thundered — straight into Lily Briscoe and William Bankes. He quivered; he shivered." [56]

---

[54] Ibid. p. 203.
[55] Ibid. p. 49.
[56] "To the Lighthouse" p. 52.

Her musical consciousness expands; she no longer limits it to suggestive harmonic structure, or, as in her first novel, to an objective exposition of the composers. Music becomes synthetic in her thoughts, molding her images as profoundly as her rhythmic style. "And now as if the cleaning and the scrubbing and the scything and the mowing had drowned it there rose that half-heard melody, that intermittent music which the ear half catches but lets fall; a bark, a bleat; irregular, intermittent, yet somehow related; the hum of an insect, the tremor of cut grass, dissevered yet somehow belonging; the jar of a dor beetle, the squeak of a wheel, loud, low, but mysteriously related; which the ear strains to bring together and is always on the verge of harmonising but they are never quite heard, never fully harmonised, and at last, in the evening, one after another the sounds die out, and the harmony falters, and silence falls." [57]

Musical themes are carried through, echoed with renewed suggestiveness, as in a fugue. A scarf is perhaps the most vital melody in the composition of the novel. It is first introduced lightly, insignificantly: "What was the use of flinging a green Cashmere shawl over the edge of a picture frame? In two weeks it would be the colour of pea-soup." [58] But there is a note of fatalism which even now distinguishes the theme. It recurs again later, modulated, intensified, given reflected life. Mrs. Ramsay takes "the green shawl off the picture frame" [59] and goes to walk with her husband. The theme is played twice with little variation: "She folded the green shawl about her shoulders." [60] The note of fatalism is later recaught with deep intimations of death. The shawl is wrapped over a boar's skull in a bedroom, that the children may sleep without terror. " 'Well then', said Mrs. Ramsay, 'we will cover it up', and they all watched her go to the chest of drawers, and open the little drawers quickly one after another, and not seeing anything that would do, she quickly took her own shawl off and wound it round the skull, round and round and round, and then she came back to Cam and laid her head almost flat on the pillow beside Cam's and said how lovely it looked now; how the fairies would love it; it was like a bird's nest; it was like a beautiful mountain such as she had seen abroad, with valleys and flowers and bells ringing and birds singing and little goats and antelopes . . ." [61] The shawl has

---

[57] Ibid p. 218.
[58] Ibid. p. 47.
[59] Ibid. p. 104.
[60] Ibid. p. 104.
[61] "To the Lighthouse" p. 177.

changed death into a poetic vision, yet beneath it lies the terrible reality: the skull, death. The theme of the scarf wavers between factual sincerity and illusion, and then reaches its climax as the symbol of life in the house's decay. "Once in the middle of the night with a roar, with a rupture, as after centuries of quiescence, a rock rends itself from the mountain and hurtles crashing into the valley, one fold of the shawl loosened and swung to and fro." [62]

Like the shawl, a knife-blade is used as a leit-motif. The professor's son James, longs for a knife to kill his father who represents for him tyranny. James is another Stephan Daedalus, at heroic odds with the forces of life. Both are sullen, ungovernable, ready to fly at their fathers. The knife is their weapon of freedom. While Stephen is nicknamed, "Kinch the knife-blade", James has a knife-blade fixation. "A rope seemed to bind him there, and his father had knotted it and he could only escape by taking a knife and plunging it . . ." [63] All through the last chapter come the words, played as the Wagnerian motif, "to resist tyranny to the death". Like the knife-blade theme, other characters are even conceived as having melodies peculiar to themselves. So Lily "tried to start the tune of Mrs. Ramsay in her head." [64]

Music, as an aesthetic and ideologic medium, is supplemented by painting. The external frame of "To the Lighthouse" is like a static canvas, with immobile chiaroscuro settings. "The Window" the first chapter is called, like the descriptive title below a painted scene. And through the whole chapter, this window forms the setting, enclosing Mrs. Ramsay, a typical Virginia Woolf figure of the Great Mother, reading a book of fairy-tales to her son James. All other life passes by that window, remolded by it like forms changed in the shadow of a tree. Reflecting Mrs. Dalloway, Mrs. Ramsay is the spirit of earth, attracting all about her, with magnetic urgency. She sits at the window with her child, looking out at the sea and the distant lighthouse, like a Renaissance painting of the Mother of God.

The importance which the possibilities of painting have assumed for Virginia Woolf is observed in her choice of a woman painter as one of her most profound characters in the novel. It is in painting that she attempts to objectify the problems which have disturbed her; from all the dark flowingness of time, to create one shape, one completed moment snatched from eternity. To Lily, hurling her questions at the universe, painting and art

---

[62] Ibid p. 201.
[63] Ibid. p. 288.
[64] Ibid. p. 80.

hold a possible answer; they are suggestive mediums, just as for the normal woman, bearing sons holds a cosmic intimation. She pieces together her memories like a scholar, before setting to work, probing them for a solution to the riddles she has projected on canvas.

Recollecting a scene on the beach with Mrs. Ramsay and Charles Tansley, the Nick Greene who murmurs destructively, "women can't paint, women can't write", [65] she recreates the past "almost like a work of art". " 'Like a work of art', she repeated, looking from her canvas to the drawing-room steps and back again. She must rest for a moment. And resting, looking from one to the other vaguely, the old question which traversed the sky of the soul perpetually, the vast, the general question which was apt to particularise itself at such moments as these, when she released faculties that had been on the strain, stood over her, paused over her, darkened over her. What is the meaning of life? That was all — a simple question; one that tended to close in on one with years. The great revelation had never come. The great revelation perhaps never did come. Instead there were little daily miracles, illuminations, matches struck unexpectedly in the dark; here was one. This, that, and the other; herself and Charles Tansley and the breaking wave; Mrs. Ramsay bringing them together; Mrs. Ramsay saying 'Life stand still here'; Mrs. Ramsay making of the moment something permanent (as in another sphere Lily herself tried to make of the moment something permanent) — this was of the nature of a revelation. In the midst of chaos there was shape; this eternal passing and flowing (she looked at the clouds going and the leaves shaking) was struck into stability. Life stand still here, Mrs. Ramsay said. 'Mrs. Ramsay! Mrs. Ramsay!' she repeated. She owed this revelation to her." [66]

Maturity has brought this "revelation" to Virginia Woolf; "in the midst of chaos there was shape", moments when life becomes symbolic, when it stands still, a tangible form reflecting and explaining everything. It is painting which has brought this explanation of life, painting with its defined object and its limitations of static time. It is painting which creates a satisfying form within the uncertain fluency of life.

Into her writing, she infuses now painting and music, two arts distinct from her own. Characteristic of her mature thought and style, she combines structure with rhythm, shape with dark flowingness, and permanency in space with the flux of time.

---

[65] Ibid. p. 77.
[66] Ibid. p. 249.

"THE WAVES" — THE RHYTHM OF CONFLICTS.

A law of polarity, of conflicts as irreconcilable, as endless as night and day, reverberates through all Virginia Woolf's writing and reaches ultimate expression in "The Waves". It is her final solution to her problem of style and her riddle of life. No truth is absolute, no style supreme.

She has perceived in her struggles, the necessity of both elements, their unquestionable truth. Recognizing the duality of life, she erects no single overwhelming standards, no damning proofs. Lacking the urgent need to negate the truths of others, she lacks also the need to point the way. Artistically and morally, she is content to observe the conflict of two forces as teleological, and in their necessary being, as good. Her struggle between the two inimical poles of style, her recognition of the need for their existence, their vital truths, has molded her philosophy of life. If integrity shows her which force, which pole she must select for herself, tolerance holds her from repudiating its counterpart. "One must put aside antipathies and jealousies" in reading a poem whose style is antithetic to her own. "One must have patience and infinite care . . . Nothing", in this polarity, "is to be rejected in fear or horror." [1] Significantly she notes the deviations from her own critical formulas, from the forces she has selected for herself. "There are no commas or semi-colons. The lines do not run in convenient lengths." [2] Objectively, she marks the lack of rhythm, and notes the disruption of her own rhetorical devices, without censure. "Much is sheer nonsense. One must be sceptical, but throw caution to the winds and when the door opens accept absolutely." [3] Tolerance of high order, to accept absolutely. But it is the tolerance of past oppression. Having suffered herself, she recoils from complete negations. Desperately she desires to accept all the values in an organic concept of life.

"Don't you feel that life's a perpetual conflict?" [4] she had written in her first novel. And in "The Waves", symbolic title of the rhythm of life, she repeats and perfects this philosophy of conflict. Six different characters, three men and three women, struggle against the amorphous collectivity of the waves to create form, to attain one moment of rested perfection. They resolve to hew their own identity, like a Rodin, within the formless massive substance of life. Like a Bible of Creation, the "Waves" describes the evolution of their lives; their childhood, where a sponge of water pressed above their heads is symbolic of the breath of life. Their

---

[1] [2] [3] "The Waves" p. 216.
[4] "The Voyage Out" p. 45.

struggle for identity begins; physical, sensuous at first, they belong completely to earth. But with the need for words, identity asserts itself. The terrible realization is immediate; nature remains unaltered; it is only man who modulates her image by his own conceits. Each man seeks a different way through which to beat against the universe. The realization of this egoistic identity, of a different nose and different thoughts and sensibilities, is as painful as it is strange. " 'I am myself, not Neville,' " Bernard exclaims, " 'a wonderful discovery'." [5] But " 'We suffered terribly as we became separate bodies' ". [6] In youth, he is most clamorous for this pole of individuality; the world is to be conquered, to be impressed with his distinct form. But with the urges of sex and of marriage, individuality loses its compulsion. Two separate identities seek to merge within each other; the desire to stand alone, one self against the sky, gives way slowly to the waves, to continuity, to bearing sons. The staccatoed sharpness of individuality changes in style to harmonic rhythm: " 'And the little fierce beat — tick-tack, tick-tack — of the pulse of one's mind took on a more majestic rhythm'." [7] " 'We are the continuers, we are the inheritors,' " [8] Bernard analyzes his life, contrasting it with the friends who do not marry, refusing to surrender to the rhythm.

In their struggle for identity or their immersion in the waves, the characters personify the greater, cosmic polarity of light and darkness, of shape and ambiguity. "The Waves" is the consummation of the problems in philosophy and style which have confronted Virginia Woolf. In artistic form, it encompasses the aesthetic problem of fact versus fancy, of sober realism and feminine illusions. It recalls the earliest problem of the critic and the poet; and denotes the divergence in the two borrowed mediums of painting and music. In philosophy, it is the struggle for individuality, of man against the masses. The problem of time is implicit, the Bergsonian distinction between the measured time of the waves and the fitful time of the creative consciousness. The urge to make "life stand still", the perfect moment abstracted from infinity, is restated with the fundamental urge to hew one form out of chaos. It is a return to the original struggle between light and darkness, order and confusion.

The aesthetic crises through which she has progressed, are thus, with urgent clarity, reanimated in "The Waves". Two poets are presented, Bernard and Neville, to personify the faction of

---

[5] "The Waves" p. 262.

[6] Ibid. p. 264.

[7] Ibid. p. 283.

[8] Ibid. p. 283.

romanticism and classicism. Bernard revels in subjective imagery, arbitrary and unselective; Neville in Roman precision and absolute concept of beauty and truth. Bernard is like young Orlando, the emotional, all-observant phase of Virginia Woolf's character. Bernard is sensuously alive to nature, to people, to his environment, but it is through his fancy rather than his eye alone. Like Virginia Woolf, objects fascinate him as they recall past associations and are convertable into literary conceits. "Up they bubble — images. 'Like a camel', . . . 'a vulture'. The camel is a vulture; the vulture a camel; for Bernard is dangling wire, loose, but seductive. Yes, for when he talks, when he makes his foolish comparison, a lightness comes over one. One floats, too, as if one were that bubble; one is freed; I have escaped, one feels." [9]

The "bubble" is the imprint of Virginia Woolf's self-consciousness. Though she justifies images, seeing in them the release of pent emotions, she is conscious also of the argument against them — her perception of polarity. Style-conscious, she acknowledges the unsolidity of many of her images, absurdly broken by the mere touch of reality. Innately visionary, she experiences the constant struggle for a deeper truth. " 'Like' and 'like' and 'like' — but what is the thing that lies beneath the semblance of the thing?" [10]

Where Bernard is rhapsodic and darkly symbolic, Neville is in love with the unclouded daylight of an Italian sky. His is the southern clarity, repelling Bernard's northern romanticism. He is the least Christian, the most Hellenic of the characters, desiring a perfection such as the Greeks had known. Admitting of life and its disorders, he seeks the Greek harmony, the beauty in nature and the vital present.

" 'In a world which contains the present moment,' said Neville, 'why discriminate? Nothing should be named lest by so doing we change it. Let it exist, this bank, this beauty, and I, for one instant, steeped in pleasure. The sun is hot. I see the river, I see trees specked and burnt in the autumn sunlight. Boats float past, through the red, through the green. Far away a bell tolls, but not for death. There are bells that ring for life. A leaf falls, from joy. Oh, I am in love with life! Look how the willow shoots its fine sprays into the air! Look how through them a boat passes, filled with indolent, with unconscious, with powerful young men. They are listening to the gramophone; they are eating fruit out of paper bags. They are tossing the skins of bananas, which then sink eel like, into the river. All they do is beautiful. There are

---

[9] "The Waves" p. 40.
[10] Ibid. p. 176.

cruets behind them and ornaments; their rooms are full of oars and oleographs but they have turned all to beauty." [11]

Of the varied characters, Neville is the humanist, the T. S. Eliot in the modern classic-romantic antithesis. He detests all vagueness and fitful connotations; he recoils from sentimentality. Reflecting the younger Virginia Woolf, influenced by the rhetoricians, he seeks the classic peaks of structure. "That would be a glorious life, to addict oneself to perfection, to follow the curve of the sentence wherever it might lead." [12] Like Rodney of "Night and Day" he is a lover of Roman ratiocination. He seeks an order implicit in form: "Everything must be done to rebuke the horror of deformity. Let us read writers of Roman severity and virtue, let us seek perfection through the sand." [13]

This desire for perfection is counterbalanced in Bernard's more feminine aesthetics and aspect of life. He lacks Neville's sense of firm, logical sequence. His are the irrational, chaotic experiences of life: "Arrows of sensation strike from my spine, but without order." [14] Life for him is a stippled inlay of the observations of little things. He is captured by the immediate image, distracted by the haphazard accidents of life.

Poetic, like Virginia Woolf, his irrelevant and unordered words are his peculiar weapon: " 'It is curious how, at every crisis, some phrase which does not fit insists upon coming to the rescue — the penalty of living in an old civilization with a notebook' ". [15] Words, mosaical.y lovely, are his offering to life. " 'I am wrapped round with phrases, like damp straw; I glow, phosphorescent. And each of you feels when I speak, "I am lit up. I am glowing" ' ". [16] Again like Virginia Woolf, he is conscious of the limitations of his words and images, of his romantic lawlessness. " 'I am apt to be deflected. I make stories. I twist up toys out of anything. A girl sits at a cottage door; she is waiting; for whom? Seduced, or not seduced? The headmaster sees the hole in the carpet. He sighs. His wife, drawing her fingers through the waves of her still abundant hair, reflects — et cetera. Waves of hands, hesitations at street corners, someone dropping a cigarette into the gutter — all are stories. But which is the true story? That I do not know. Hence I keep my phrases hung like clothes in a cupboard, waiting for someone to wear them. Thus waiting, thus speculating, making this note and then another, I do not cling to

[11] "The Waves" p. 87.
[12] Ibid. p. 94.
[13] Ibid. p. 196.
[14] Ibid. p. 170.
[15] Ibid. p. 200.
[16] Ibid. p. 237.

life. I shall be brushed like a bee from a sunflower. My philosophy, always accumulating, welling up moment by moment, runs
like quicksilver a dozen ways at once' ". [17]

Representing the two poles of literary style, the two phases
of Virginia Woolf's conflict, neither Bernard nor Neville surpasses
the other. Neither one can proclaim that his is the absolute style,
nor boast that his poetic recreation of life is the true one for
mankind. Signally, both poets fall short of immortality; an
intimation, sub-conscious perhaps, of the author's personal fear.

It is wavering integrity which impedes Neville, tragically
caused by the dualism of his nature. Over-conscious, he oscillates
constantly and in hesitating, loses his sincerity. The "flaw in the
center" which had impelled the decay of women's creation, is his
bar to greatness too. " 'Now begins to rise in me the familiar
rhythm; words that have lain dormant now lift, now toss their
crests, and fall and rise, and fall and rise again. I am a poet, yes.
Surely I am a great poet. Boats and youth passing and distant
trees, 'the falling fountains of the pendant trees'. I see it all.
I am inspired. My eyes fill with tears. Yet even as I feel this, I
lash my frenzy higher and higher. It foams. It becomes artificial,
insincere. Words and words and words, how they gallop — how
they lash their long manes and tails, but for some fault in me I
cannot give myself to their backs; I cannot fly with them,
scattering women and string bags. There is some flaw in me —
some fatal hesitancy, which, if I pass it over, turns to foam and
falsity' ". [18]

And just as Neville, the classicist, fails through "some flaw",
"some fatal hesitancy", so Bernard, the romanticist, fails too.
Within the tremendous bounds of a law of polarity, are scales and
gradations for the weak and the great. Bernard's "charm and flow
of language" is enfeebled by the very blunders of his romanticism.
Actively sensitive, like Virginia Woolf, to all impressions, he knows
little selectivity or rigid form. "I am astonished, as I draw the
veil off things with words, how much, how infinitely more than
I can say, I have observed. More and more bubbles into my mind
as I talk, images and images. This, I say to myself, is what I need;
why, I ask, can I not finish the letter that I am writing? For my
room is always scattered with unfinished letters." [19]

The tragic failure of the romanticists may be symbolized in the
room of unfinished letters, unfinished because consciousness has

---

[17] "The Waves" p. 238.
[18] Ibid. p. 88.
[19] Ibid. p. 90.

come before the end and reason has shown the flaws in imagery
and rhythm. The fear that comes as soon as inspiration has waned,
the fear of being insincere, which obstructs Neville, is again the
grim destroyer. The great inner compulsion, which necessitates
completion of a work, recedes; faith is lost. Sensitive to criticism,
Bernard loses his integrity. It is significantly Neville, in his
counter sensibilities, who analyzes Bernard's failure. He perceives
"a certain effort, an extravagance in his phrase". Percival, he
notes " 'feels bored; I too feel bored. Bernard at once perceives
that we are bored. I detect a certain effort, an extravagance in his
phrase, as if he said 'Look!' but Percival says 'No'. For he is
always the first to detect insincerity; and is brutal in the extreme.
The sentence tails off feebly. Yes, the appalling moment has
come when Bernard's power fails him and there is no longer any
sequence and he sags and twiddles a bit of string and falls silent,
gaping as if about to burst into tears. Among the tortures and
devastations of life is this then — our friends are not able to
finish their stories' ". [20]

In all its sharp antitheses, the struggle which has marked
Virginia Woolf's development is presented. In Bernard and
Neville she erects the poles of her literary conflict. Currents are
set up between them, but all attemps to establish a superiority,
fail. Greatness, she perceives, is determined not by classic or
romantic mannerisms, but by a deeper recognition of human
values, molded but not subjugated by form. It is the mark of
Virginia Woolf's organic concept of life, that she concludes an end-
lessness in conflicts. As long as there is night and day, light and
darkness, there will be antithetic stylists, inimical poets and
negating critics.

The conclusion that there is no absolute truth in either fact
or fancy, structural or rhythmic form, enables her to employ both
styles without self-consciousness or doubt. The conceits and lyrical
cadences which marked "The Voyage Out" are restored, supplemented by the intellectual, clarified structure of "Night and Day".
No compromise is struck between them; both are used to frame
two distinct moods. Melodic lyricism, however, far outweighs
architectural sophistication. Fluidity is dominant: " 'I flutter.
I ripple. I stream like a plant in the river, flowing this way,
flowing that way' ". [21]   Yet concurrent with this rhythmic
emotionality is the structure of thought: "the fringe of my
intelligence floating unattached caught those distant sensations
which after a time the mind draws in and works upon." [22]

[20] "The Waves" p. 40.
[21] Ibid. p. 110.
[22] Ibid. p. 272.

The laws of mathematics, though less a part of Virginia Woolf's nature than the laws of music, throw added light upon the Faustean "two souls which dwell within my bosom". Orchestral music is envisioned in the symbols of mathematics, of abstract thought. This is not the meaning of life, but the refuge, the surcease from the desperate, hopeless search.

"There is a square; there is an oblong. The players take the square and place it upon the oblong. They place it very accurately; they make a perfect dwelling-place. Very little is left outside. The structure is now visible; what is inchoate is here stated; we are not so various or so mean; we have made oblongs and stood them upon squares. This is our triumph; this is our consolation.

" 'The sweetness of this content overflowing runs down the walls of my mind, and liberates understanding. Wander no more, I say; this is the end. The oblong has been set upon the square; the spiral is on top' ". [23]

Reanimating conflicts, "The Waves" gives profound expression to the divergence between painting and music when used by a writer. Just as, within the polarity of romanticism and classicism, Virginia Woolf tends to seek out one pole, so in the antipodal borrowed arts, she tends towards that of music. The musical technicalities which had characterized especially "Jacob's Room" and "To the Lighthouse" are again applied, with increasing simulation of the opera. Like an overture before each act, a descriptive preface ushers in the chapters. With poetic symbols and extreme romanticism, these prefaces foreshadow the action which is to follow. They unfold, with inner sequence, the normal day, tracing the movement of the sun. The symbol is immediate; the one day is the microcosmic reflection of the life of the characters, the evolution of the sun, their rise and fall. Their childhood is implied by dawn, and in the few chosen objects which compose the prefaces, all their mental torments, their longings for identity or immersion, their moments of joy or resignation are suggested. Human changes are portrayed as the six characters mature, reflecting age the slope of the sun. The book opens in the uncertain greyness between darkness and dawn, symbolic of early childhood.

"The sun had not yet risen. The sea was indistinguishable from the sky, except that the sea was slightly creased as if a cloth had wrinkles in it. Gradually as the sky whitened a dark line lay on the horizon dividing the sea from the sky and the grey cloth became barred with thick strokes moving, one after another,

---

[23] Ibid. p. 176.

beneath the surface, following each other, pursuing each other, perpetually.

"As they neared the shore each bar rose, heaped itself, broke and swept a thin veil of white water across the sand. The wave paused, and then drew out again, sighing like a sleeper, whose breath comes and goes unconsciously. Gradually the dark bar on the horizon became clear as if the sediment in an old wine-bottle had sunk and left the glass green. Behind it, too, the sky cleared as if the white sediment there had sunk, or as if the arm of a woman couched beneath the horizon had raised a lamp and flat bars of white, green and yellow spread across the sky like the blades of a fan. Then she raised her lamp higher and the air seemed to become fibrous and to tear away from the green surface flickering and flaming in red and yellow fibres like the smoky fire that roars from a bonfire. Gradually the fibres of the burning bonfire were fused into one haze, one incandescence which lifted the weight of the woolen grey sky on top of it and turned it to a million atoms of soft blue. The surface of the sea slowly became transparent and lay rippling and sparkling until the dark stripes were almost rubbed out. Slowly the arm that held the lamp raised it higher and then higher until a broad flame became visible; an arc of fire burnt on the rim of the horizon, and all round it the sky blazed gold.

"The light struck upon the trees in the garden, making one leaf transparent and then another. One bird chirped high up; there was a pause; another chirped lower down." (This trick of contrasting upward and downward motion is constant throughout Virginia Woolf's later writing, typical of her aspect of the rhythm of life). "The sun sharpened the walls of the house, and rested like the tip of a fan upon a white blind and made a blue finger-print of shadow under the leaf by the bedroom window. The blind stirred slightly, but all within was dim and unsubstantial. The birds sang their blank melody outside." [24]

It is the overture to childhood. The hidden sun, the blending of sky and sea are symbolic of that stage of half-trauma where the child is still vaguely identified with his mother. Like the slow sun-rise, the child breaks from the infinitude and darkness of his birth. The poetic imagery of the prefaces is veiled with deep mysticism; there is little clarity, little objectification. The effect is that of a shimmering network through which objects are seen in fragments quickly lost. No vision is made plastic; there is an interweaving of figures and sensations. The images want distinction, natural in the poet's apprehension of an organic, amorphous flow of time.

---

[24] Ibid. p. 5.

The chapters are founded upon leit-motifs barely variated from the opening pages to their close. Each of the six characters is presented with a unique concept of life, abstracted in a symbolic image or a typifying phrase. The six appear like mystic poets seeing visions whose symbolism gains comprehension as the characters mature. These esoteric visions are the expression, the dialogue of the consciousness. Sounded in early childhood, they are repeated throughout, becoming the motifs through which their thoughts are entered upon the stage. There is no direct discourse; the lyricist Virginia Woolf recoils again from dramaturgy. Soliloquies are juxtaposed, related only by an external semblance of conversation. The desire to write such a novel is found stated in her earliest work: " 'I want to write a novel about Silence,' " says Terence; " 'the things people don't say. But the difficulty is immense' ". [25] It needed true integrity and self-confidence for Virginia Woolf to create in her last novel what she had sought for in her first. It needed maturity. This is the language of the inner life; of the half-conscious torments and desires. It is one long self-expression; the ego is unchained. Exploring again the stream of consciousness, the novelist does not fall back, as in "Mrs. Dalloway", upon long prose expositions, but imitates the continuum of conversation in the psychic realm. It is a conversation like the consciousness itself, stripped of dramatic flesh, exposing the rich intricacies of the nervous system. The characters speak parallel to each other as though through nerve reactions, rather than through a tangible stimulus of words. Dispensing with all action and artistic motivation, the six are introduced together. In childhood the play begins, all perceiving the images that remain their vision of life:

" 'I see a ring,' said Bernard, 'hanging above me. It quivers and hangs in a loop of light.'

" 'I see a slab of pale yellow,' said Susan, 'spreading away until it meets a purple stripe.'

" 'I hear a sound,' said Rhoda, 'cheep, chirp; cheep, chirp; going up and down.'

" 'I se a globe,' said Neville. 'hanging down in a drop against the enormous flanks of some hill.'

" 'I see a crimson tassel,' said Jinny, "Twisted with gold threads.'

" 'I hear something stamping,' said Louis. 'A great beast's foot is chained. It stamps, and stamps, and stamps.'

" 'Look at the spider's web on the corner of the balcony,' said Bernard. 'It has beads of water on it, drops of white light.'

[25] "The Voyage Out" p. 262.

" 'The leaves are gathered round the window like pointed ears,' said Susan.

" 'A shadow falls on the path,' said Louis, 'like an elbow bent.'

" 'Islands of light are swimming on the grass,' said Rhoda. 'They have fallen through the trees.'

" 'The bird's eyes are bright in the tunnels between the leaves,' said Neville.

" 'The stalks are covered with harsh, short hairs,' said Jinny, 'and drops of water have stuck to them.'

" 'A caterpillar is curled in a green ring,' said Susan, 'notched with blunt feet.'

" 'The grey-shelled snail draws across the path and flattens the blades behind him,' said Rhoda.

" 'And burning lights from the window-panes flash in and out on the grasses,' said Louis.

" 'Stones are cold to my feet,' said Neville. 'I feel each one, round or pointed, separately.'

" 'The back of my hand burns,' said Jinny, 'but the palm is clammy and damp with dew.'

" 'Now the cock crows like a spurt of hard, red water in the white tide,' said Bernard.

" 'Birds are singing up and down and in and out all around us,' said Susan.

" 'The beast stamps; the elephant with its foot chained; the great brute on the beach stamps,' said Louis." [26]

With wide eyes staring outwards, these children see little but their inner souls. Yet no children speak as they do; Virginia Woolf has not revealed the consciousness of the child but of the mystic visionary. These first images are not changed as the characters mature, but remain the touchstone of the "true self" which Orlando and Virginia Woolf have struggled to determine. The six appear in all their marked polarity as variations not only of Virginia Woolf's observations, but with necessary modifications, of the polarity of her own character. Bernard embodies her poetic romanticism, Neville her conflicting struggle for classic formal order. In Rhoda she depicts her flight from reality to a realm of fantastic loveliness; in Louis, her longing for success to manifest, at least to the world, that she has unchained "the great beast's foot', freed herself from the tyranny of the waves. The fulfilled woman, Mrs. Woolf, inseparable from earth, is idealized in Susan, while Jinny reflects her sense of

---

[26] "The Waves" p. 7.

flowingness, the delight in partaking of the irrational rhythm
of life.

Two great divisions become apparent, two phases of human
thought. On the one hand are the characters who seek a Reason
behind the universe, an order divined by the intellect. On the
other, are the characters, intuitive and more poetic, who conceive
life as an incessant rise and fall of waves. For them there is
no higher meaning, no absolute Reason within and beyond their
own existence. It is in such a philosophy of irrational continuity
that Virginia Woolf, as poet and woman, believes. Yet in her
endless struggle for the meaning of life, traces of a search for
some cause, some higher force, create in her a philosophic
conflict, analogous to the conflict into which she divides her
characters.

Life is poetically symbolized in the waves; the characters
distinguished as they accept the apparently meaningless rhythm or
seek imposed order. All of them search for happiness, each through
his own vision, his own reaction to the waves. It is Susan who
seeks the "natural happiness" implicit in merging herself within
the endless organism of nature. " 'I shall never have anything
but natural happiness. It will almost content me. I shall go to
bed tired. I shall lie like a field bearing crops in rotation; in
the summer heat will dance over me; in the winter I shall be
cracked with the cold. But heat and cold will follow each other
naturally without my willing or unwilling. My children will carry
me on; their teething, their crying, their going to school and
coming back will be like the waves of the sea under me' ". [27]
The eternal movement holds for Susan the meaning of life. She
has no desire to impose her will upon the waves; she is too
sensible of the futility in defying the stupendous rhythm. Hers
is a cosmic order in which her own sharp identity is lost. It is
Louis, supersensitive, who seeks a volitional order, a personal
superiority, to compensate for his "neatness", his "Australian
accent", aggravated idiosyncrasies barring him from the "protective
waves of the ordinary." [28] Being antisocial, he revolts against
the amorphous rhythm: " 'I will reduce you to order' " [29] is his
cry against the irrelevant details in the mosaic of life. It is his
flaunt against the "hats bobbing up and down", the opening and
shutting of the door, "the hesitations at counters; and the words
that trail drearily without meaning; I will reduce you to order' ". [30]

---

[27] "The Waves" p. 142.
[28] Ibid. p. 101.
[29] Ibid. p. 102.
[30] Ibid. p. 102.

Inseparable from this problem of identity against the waves, is the problem of time, a constant throughout her novels. The one moment consummate of all time, is sought for, despaired of, and even if ultimately experienced, returns, with the inexorable law of the waves, back into the dark massive flowingness of time. In the conflict between the one identified moment of light and the dark progress of eternity, lies the Bergson-Orlando discord between "time in the mind and time in the clock." Neville, "who had been thinking with the unlimited time of the mind, which stretches in a flash from Shakespeare to ourselves, poked the fire and began to live by that other clock which marks the approach of a particular person. From the myriads of mankind and all time past he had chosen one person, one moment in particular." [31]

Against the confusion of eternity, he erects one unity. In the arbitrary order he imposes upon time, the conflict of chaos and shape, the great conflict of "The Waves" is thus reflected. Neville, like Louis and like Lily of "To the Lighthouse", seeks to objectify the chaos, to pierce it with light. But upon him, as upon all the characters, hangs the shadow of primal darkness, ridiculing their activity, almost negating their lives.

" 'Our separate drops are dissolved; we are extinct, lost in the abysses of time, in the darkness' ". [32] The quests for identity, for classic order, for light, for the supreme moment, are rendered futile in a pause of silence, an effigy of the long nothingness. " 'As silence falls,' " Bernard says, " 'I am dissolved utterly and become featureless and scarcely to be distinguished from another. It does not matter. What matters?' " [33] Embedded in English futilitarianism, the characters for a time lose their driving will for power, upon which Freud has laid man's struggle for happiness. Viewing their lives against the setting of eternity, they become apathetic to the urge for fame. Kings and paupers fall alike into the great oblivion of time: "how strange it seems to set against the whirling abysses of infinite space a little figure with a golden tea-pot on his head. Soon one recovers belief in figures: but not at once in what they put on their heads. Our English past — one inch of light. Then people put teapots on their heads and say, 'I am a King!' No I try to recover, as we walk, the sense of time, but with that streaming darkness in my eyes I have lost my grip . . . What do we oppose, with this random flicker of light in us that we call brain and feeling, how can we do battle against this flood; what has permanence? Our

[31] "The Waves" p. 299.
[32] Ibid. p. 246.
[33] Ibid. p. 245.

lives too stream away, down the unlighted avenues, past the strip of time, unidentified." [34]

Power, majesty, identity are all illusions, all futile, at this stage of middling life. The waves are impervious. Characteristic of her womanhood, Virginia Woolf surrenders herself more and more to their amorphous rhythm, to the periodicity of sleeping and waking, of living and dying. The desire to impose order is "a mistake . . . a convenience, a lie. There is always deeply below it . . . a rushing stream of broken dreams, nursery rhymes, street cries, half-finished sentences and sights." [35]

She negates for a time all the characters who seek to subjugate the waves into an order in which they alone are supreme. Neville's cry, " 'Oppose ourselves to this illimitable chaos . . . this formless imbecility' " [36] is immediately softened. The beauty in endless nature, in this very chaos, makes man seem ugly, insignificant with petty lusts. The struggle for the reins with which to govern life, directing it with kingly power, is subdued. She longs no longer to order the waves but to be ordered within them.

Meaningless, aimless, it is this dull acquiescence to the rhythm of life which makes men futilitarians. Apparently, all is vain; only a "memento mori", the medieval refuge remains. In the final judgment of all their lives, Bernard, aged, a failure to himself, reflects " 'How we surrender, how we submit to the stupidity of nature' ". [37] The youthful struggle for identity has crumbled. He is certain of what in childhood had been mooted: "satiety and doom" — death. " 'I cried then with a sudden conviction of complete desertion, Now there is nothing. No fin to break the waste of this immeasurable sea. Life has destroyed me' ". [38]

" 'How then does light return to the earth after the eclipse of the sun? Miraculously. Frailly . . . There is a spark there. Next moment a flush of dun." [39] So Bernard ends not in disillusion; light returns to him in the need to struggle, in the exertion of power, in the search for identity and freedom. In opposition alone can he find happiness. Not in solving the conflict but in the very struggle, life fulfills its meaning. " 'Fight! Fight!' . . . . It is the effort and the struggle, it is the perpetual warfare, it is

[34] "The Waves" p. 248.
[35] Ibid. p. 279.
[36] Ibid. p. 246.
[37] Ibid. p. 294.
[38] Ibid. p. 311.
[39] Ibid. p. 313.

the shattering and piecing together — this is the daily battle, defeat or victory, the absorbing pursuit' ". [40]

The philosophy of futilitarianism has been defeated once more by activity. The body's urge for action has rejuvenated the spirit of youth. It has saved the poet from nihilism and spiritual apathy. "The Waves", a Vulgate of existence, ends not in death, but in dawn. The struggle against death is reanimated, the rhythm of night and day, of life and death is retrieved.

"There is a sense of the break of day . . . . Another day; another Friday; another twentieth of March, January, or September. Another general awakening. The stars draw back and are extinguished. The bars deepen themselves between the waves. The film of mist thickens on the fields. A redness gathers on the roses, even on the pale rose that hangs by the bedroom window. A bird chirps. Cottagers light their early candles. Yes, this is the eternal renewal, the incessant rise and fall and fall and rise again.

"And in me too the wave rises. It swells; it arches its back. I am aware once more of a new desire, something rising beneath me like the proud horse whose rider first spurs and then pulls him back. What enemy do we now perceive advancing against us, you whom I ride now, as we stand pawing this stretch of pavement? It is death. Death is the enemy. It is death against whom I ride with my spear couched and my hair flying back like a young man's, like Percival's, when he galloped in India. I strike spurs into my horse. Against you I will fling myself, unvanquished and unyielding, O Death!' "

"The waves broke on the shore." [41]

To the last note, the conflict is sounded. Man must struggle for freedom, struggle against death. And yet, inexorably, the waves rise and fall; death is the one law of life.

It is the constancy of antitheses, the rhythm of conflicts, which determines Virginia Woolf's philosophy as well as her style. It is the two weights upon the balance which she sees struggling for supremacy. Hers is the philosophy of the earliest primitives a philosophy to which all others revert; out of darkness came light, out of death, life. She sees all things, like a Noah's ark, in pairs of like and unlike, of classicist and romanticist, of man and woman, of night and day. There is no synthetic solution to their opposition; health lies in being a man or a woman, not a compromise between them.

---

[40] Ibid. p. 295.
[41] "The Waves" p. 324.

THE WILL TO CREATE AS A WOMAN

Influenced by men in the beginnning of her career, Virginia Woolf evolves, with irresistible force, the woman within her. A womanly love of details subverts the more rigid sense of form; her novels have a feminine expansiveness, an apparent irrelevancy which is truer to life than to art. She has little of the logic and restraint called manly; her sensibilities, her emotions, her philosophy of life are normally feminine. Freed from the shame of her sex, a shame which drove other women to hide behind male pseudonyms, she explores her femininity and within it, creates her style.

She accepts the tradition that women cannot think abstractly, that their scope is smaller than man's. It is this very limitation which she consecrates, availing herself of the smaller scope, of the petty and the concrete. Seeking always the meaning of life, its great profundities, she has discovered that a mention of their names alone, of immortality or God or death, is no persuasion of their truth, no crucible of the profundity of her work. In life itself, the recurring wonder of finding these deepest realities reflected even in trivialities, impresses her; she converts her observation into art. She particularizes truth; the meaning of life she detects in "waves of hands, hesitations at street corners", in "a nightingale, who sings among the trampling feet." [1] Peculiarly feminine, she finds more vividness and perhaps more truth in these small symbolic details. Philosophic Latinities, pale and abstract, are often so suggestive, she feels, that they lose distinction and suggest nothing. All must be concrete, and if not personal, at least specific. " 'I have little aptitude for reflection,' " says Bernard, " ' I require the concrete in everything. It is only so that I lay hands upon the world' ". [2]

It is as though a new realm had been opened in literature, the world of women, correlated to the other longer established one of men, and yet remaining peculiarly distinct. Both seek the same finalities of love, reality and death, but it is as if two unique towers had been erected and the men peered through one telescope and the women through another. Fundamental differences, ultimately acknowledged by man and woman, now can be developed. The problem of describing the world she sees, uninhibited by convention, is one of the first difficulties Virginia Woolf confronts. From the start, her ideal is to create as a woman: in her earliest novel she pronounces Jane Austen "incomparably

---

[1] "The Waves" p. 38.
[2] Ibid. p. 73.

the greatest female writer we possess . . . and for this reason: she does not attempt to write like a man. Every other woman does." [3] With increasing consciousness, this ideal progresses through her works, unmitigated by critical opinion, becoming less a spoken theory than the general insinuation.

The little things in life, the scarves and windows, she describes with feminine integrity; they are the things which touch women, an element of beauty in their lives. The sensory experience derived from clothes and ornamentation, may be described with the same emotional rhythm and imagery as experiences long conventionalized. An analysis of woman's sensations in a modern department store, of the awakening perceptions of desire, of envy, of hunger, or of aesthetic satisfaction, may penetrate her consciousness as poignantly as would an analysis of her love-life. These reactions demand no revolutionary experiments in expression. Yet an obsolete stye, filled with allegory or conceits, would seem little better than a comedy of anachronisms, an extravaganza in style.

In her most signal essay, "A Room of One's Own", Virginia Woolf lays down a platform in which the woman novelist can find truest expression. You must illumine your own soul with its profundities and its shallows, and its vanities and its generosities, and say what your beauty means to you or your plainness, and what is your relation to the ever-changing and turning world of gloves and shoes and stuffs swaying up and down among the faint scents that come through chemist's bottles down arcades of dress material over a floor of pseudo-marble." [4]

Sensory apperceptions are as vital, evoked by an apothecary, as those evoked by nature. The irresistible attraction of a shopping-center is a value rarely denied, though often ridiculed or overlooked by masculine writers. Mrs. Dalloway's reaction to the London shopping district is denotative of her whole romantic feminine nature: "Bond Street fascinated her; Bond Street early in the morning in the season; its flags flying; its shops; . . . . a few pearls; salmon on an ice-block." [5] In her "passion for gloves" lies a penetrating characteristic of her fastidious personality: "Her old Uncle William used to say a lady is known by her shoes and her gloves." [6]

The urge for selectivity, for choosing the proper objects as material, has been one of the moot problems of all literature.

---

[3] "The Voyage Out" p. 66.
[4] "A Room of One's Own" p. 135.
[5] "Mrs. Dalloway" p. 15.
[6] Ibid. p. 16.

Not only form changes from age to age, but the interests change too. And just as the selection from the vast soil of human potentialities, depends upon the personality of the writer, so it depends also upon his sex. Integrity is imminent; a writer is of necessity discounted if he yields weakly to dictated standards. Yet women have been expected to submit unquestioningly to the standards imposed by men, to use a form which man has evolved to suit himself, and objects which have meaning for him. "But it is obvious," Virginia Woolf writes, "that the values of women differ very often from the values which have been made by the other sex; naturally, this is so. Yet it is the masculine values that prevail. Speaking crudely, football and sport are 'important'; the worship of fashion, the buying of clothes 'trivial'. And these values are inevitably transferred from life to fiction. This is an important book, the critic assumes, because it deals with war. This is an insignificant book because it deals with the feelings of women in a drawing-room A scene in a battle-field is more important than a scene in a shop — everywhere and much more subtly the difference of value persits." [7]

The expression of feminine values, characterizes for Virginia Woolf the integrity of the woman novelist. Subjectively conscious of the power which trifling femininities may have upon the emotions, she describes the texture of a dress, its color and its style, as carefully as Wells might describe a utopian invention. More poetically than he, she infuses her details with feminine denotations. The dress becomes the symbol of the characters, marking their desires and personality. " 'This great company, all dressed in brown serge, has robbed me of my identity,' " [8] says Rhoda, in revolting unhappily against the masses. Jinny's reaction to clothes, directly following, stamps her contrasting nature. Without conflict or rebellion, she finds in clothes the very expression of herself, the means with which she makes her debut into life. In the waving of a scarf, the fluttering of a dress, she discovers her meaning in life. Attracting men, part of the lawful rhythm of the waves, she finds in these preliminaries to human intercourse, the essence of love, the quintessence of life. Through her dress, she reflects herself: " 'for winter I should like a thin dress shot with red threads that would gleam in the firelight. Then when the lamps were lit, I should put on my red dress and it would be thin as a veil, and would wind about my body, and billow out as I came into the room,

---

[7] "A Room of One's Own" p. 111 .
[8] "The Waves" p. 35.

pirouetting. It would make a flower shape as I sank down, in the middle of the room, on a gilt chair' ". [9] Just as her clothes typify Jinny's personality, so in "Jacob's Room", the dress becomes epithetic, and Sandra is repeatedly characterized, with Homeric inconography, as "veiled in white" [10] symbolic of her Grecian beauty. Her dress, her lipstick, her handkerchief, the weapons which woman employs for conquering or defending herself are, though immeasurably different from man's, no less effective. A powder-puff may be as deadly as a sword, "obliterating in its passage all the most fervent feelings of the human heart." [11]

The beauty of a well served dinner, Virginia Woolf finds can be as profound as the beauty of a sunset. The composition of a bowl of fruit, the possibilities of which had been recognized as a rich subject for painting, may obtain as well for literary description. The long tradition of household cares has made her sensitive to apparently insignificant objects. As much emotion may be aroused through the position of a fork beside a napkin, as much nervousness or satisfaction, as through the position of a tree against the sky. Design is everywhere, even the patterns of food may be symbolic of the accidents of life. " 'How strange,' said Susan, 'the little heaps of sugar look by the side of our plates. Also the mottled peelings of pears, and the plush rims to the looking-glasses. I had not seen them before. Everything is now set; everything is fixed. Bernard is engaded' ". [12] The order experienced in life as prearranged, imposes itself conceptually upon a woman's arrangement of the table. There is an awakening to the human dispensation of trifling objects, reflecting the superhuman structure of the universe.

The contemporary interest in formalism, seen as the relationship of shapes, often selects, the unimportant or the extraordinary for material and gives them new values. Seeking a flexibility between style and thought, tradition and experiment, Virginia Woolf combines her old rhetorical standards with which she had sung of nature, with this new structural formalism explicit of her interest in still-life.

Food, its colors, its form, interests her as it interests a Cezanne, for the sensuous satisfaction it obtains. In the general impulse to see complexity and loveliness in attributes before unnoticed, she describes the formal beauty in the juxtaposition of fruit, variously shaped. "Her eyes had been going in and out among the curves and shadows of the fruit, among

[9] Ibid. p. 35
[10] "Jacob's Room" p. 230; p. 249.
[11] "The Waves" p. 156.
[12] Ibid. p. 154.

the rich purples of the low-land grapes, then over the horny ridge of the shell, putting a yellow against a purple, a curved shape against a round shape, without knowing why she did it, or why, every time she did it, she felt more and more serene." [13] An aesthetic gratification induced by still-life diffuses her with the calmness which poets had been used to seek in the woods at the side of a lake.

Formal satisfaction, indigenous to this age, she supplements with the romantic associations typical of her style: "the arrangement of the grapes and pears, of the horny pink-lined shell, of the bananas, made her think of a trophy fetched from the bottom of the sea, of Neptune's banquet, of the bunch that hangs with vine leaves over the shoulder of Bacchus (in some picture), among the leopard skins and the torches lolloping red and gold . . ." [14]

Combining the culinary heritage of her sex with a romantic contemporary delight in minutiae, Virginia Woolf experiences in food not only the possibilities of aesthetic satisfaction but a deep physical pleasure. Novelist and woman, she is concerned with food as it is a primal necessity; hunger is a biologic urge of which she is not ashamed. "It is a curious fact that novelists have a way of making us believe that luncheon parties are invariably memorable for something very witty that was said, or for something very wise that was done. But they seldom spare a word for what was eaten. It is part of the novelist's convention not to mention soup and salmon and ducklings, as if soup and salmon and ducklings were of no importance whatsoever, as if nobody ever smoked a cigar or drank a glass of wine." [15] Her own characters dine luxuriously; no attic poverty entices her. With a mixture of feminine sensitivity to food and a poetic urge for conceits, she describes a meal in diction suggestive of the Cavalier poets. A dish of soles, spread with "a counterpane of the whitest cream", is branded "like the spots on the flanks of a doe". Sprouts are "foliated as rosebuds but more succulent", and a pudding, "wreathed in napkins" rises "all sugar from the waves." [16]

Just as the male novelists had often used environments which were peculiarly masculine, as battle-fields and halls for parliament, so Virginia Woolf seeks that setting which is peculiarly feminine — the room. "For women have sat indoors all these millions of years, so that by this time the very walls are permeated by their creative force." [17] The room is a fixated image throughout

---

[13] "To the Lighthouse" p. 168.
[14] Ibid. p. 151.
[15] "A Room of One's Own" p. 16.
[16] Ibid. p. 16.
[17] Ibid. p. 131.

her works; in "A *Room* of One's Own" it is the refuge for the feminine artist; the seclusion from the critic with freedom to write and think. Her women, oppressed by society, flee to their rooms as poets flee back to nature, there to find themselves. " 'I went back to my room by myself and I did — what I liked' ",[18] says Katherine of "Night and Day". It is in her room in solitude that she becomes "a creature of uncalculating passion and instinctive freedom."[19] The room, like a civilized substitute for nature, is not only the harbor for desperate flights, but is as "Jacob's *Room*" or Mrs. Dalloway's ballroom, the background for life, the stage molded by and itself molding the characters. Both men and women are seen against this setting. The room or its smaller counterpart, the railway carriage, become the sources for the material of life.

In the essay "Mr. Bennett and Mrs. Brown", "Life" in the form of the old woman Mrs. Brown, is analyzed against the background of a train compartment. It is Virginia Woolf's great complaint against the Edwardians, against Wells and Bennett and Galsworthy, that they do not see the life in the room, that they evade Mrs. Brown and look out of the window. " 'I fill my mind,' " she says through Bernard, " 'with whatever happens to be the contents of a room or a railway carriage as one fills a fountain pen in an inkpot' ".[20] Her sensitivity to the room is as vitally feminine as is her sensitivity to food and clothes. Its expression is a trenchant mark of her will to create as a woman. The rooms she observes are as varied as continental landscapes; but more subjective than nature, they are created and determined by the women who inhabit them. "The rooms differ so completely; they are calm or thunderous; open on to the sea, or, on the contrary, give on to a prison yard; are hung with washing; or alive with opals and silks; are hard as horsehair or soft as feathers — one has only to go into any room in any street for the whole of that extremely complex force of feminity to fly in one's face."[21]

Her aspect of life, the background against which she conceives her men as well as her women, projects itself into the room and the window. In the room conflicts are fought and overcome; passions or indifferences are stimulated by the walls and the atmospheric setting, just as lights and tones are brought out in a portrait by its background. At the window the room is negated; one flees, perhaps from the sofa with its associations of sex, and in looking out at the stars, grows almost sexless. The window is

---

[18] "Night and Day" p. 355.
[19] Ibid. p. 355.
[20] "The Waves" p. 73.
[21] "A Room of One's Own" p. 131.

for the poetic man or woman; it is the harbor for dreams. In the window and the room is seen the conflict of the individual against society, of the people who flee from reality and those who determine to stay, to find themselves in life. Woman as well as man is communal in the room, in the sitting or the dining room. She is seen and sees herself as a relationship. At the window she is abstracted from the whole. The window replaces the romanticist's mountain top, from which the characters, restless, unhappy, lonely, characters like Katherine and Louis, look down into the street, as the romanticists look down into the valley. They note the sounds, the passers-by. Detached from the rhythm of the room, they respond tremblingly to the symphonic rhythm of the unknown world.

The characters of Virginia Woolf's novels might be divided into those who fit into the room, who have found themselves in life, and those who stand at windows, the dreamers, the anchorites. In the room belong the great women, perfected mentally and bodily, women like Mrs. Ambrose of "The Voyage Out". It is a room conceived like the last gallery in the Louvre with its tall flawless statue in the center and around it the marble floor and velvet stools for worshippers. At the window belongs Rachel, dreaming of music, discontent with mankind, in love. The politicians, the successful novelists, and most of the scholars would fit into the room; at the window, the lovers, the spinsters and the poets who have not yet arrived.

Through a deep psychological analysis of her reactions to the room and to its people, Virginia Woolf thus attempts to make her novels irrefutably feminine, the creation of a woman. Not to flaunt her sex, not to justify or evade it artificially; her ideal is to "write as a woman but as a woman who has forgotten that she is a woman, so that her pages were full of that curious sexual quality which comes only when sex is unconscious of itself." [22] She demands no sterility, no social aberrations for the novelist; only a normal sexuality, giving blood and freshness to her creation.

She attempts to infuse this "curious sexual quality" in her writings, and in describing comparatively normal people, succeeds. "Jacob's Room" with its stippled sketches of love between mother and son, between artist and model, between husband and wife, between the wife and a lover, is filled with this feminine sexual quality. Sex permeates the book but always with feminine delicacy, verging upon Victorian innuendos. In her language itself and in her descriptions, there is no trace of obscenity; sex is described in veiled insinuations. But there is one scene slipping from

[22] "A Room of One's Own" p. 140.

the rest, where suggestiveness goes too far and becomes sentimental, ill-concealed pornography. The bedroom noises are described through the reactions of the sitting room, endowed with life. There is no censurable word uttered, only phrases, apparently innocuous, like "the door was shut"; "wood, when it creaks"; "these old houses . . . soaked in human sweat, grained with human dirt"; muffled with a sentimental personification of a letter as a mother's heart; "if the pale blue envelope lying by the biscuit-box had the feelings of a mother, the heart was torn by the little creak, the sudden stir"; with the climax, no longer concealed by poetic euphuisms: "behind the door was the obscene thing, the alarming presence." [23] She is shocked by it, "the obscene thing", she holds it off from her on prongs, shuddering even to name it. Her mind is blocked; she has lost her objectivity, that "incandescence" which she preaches so fervently for others. She falls in her attempt to write without shocking, in Victorian discreetness.

This scene in "Jacob's Room" is a fine instance of the pitfalls in her sex analysis. But she is too deeply rooted in the modern Freudian atmosphere to evade sex. As a woman, moreover, recognizing in sex a primal force in life, she is sensitive to its value in literature. In "A Room of One's Own" she preaches a utopia where the woman novelist will take her notebook into the bordels, unhindered by social criticism or her own self-consciousness. "She will not need to limit herself any longer to the respectable houses of the upper middle classes. She will go without kindness or condescension, but in the spirit of fellowship, into those small, scented rooms where sit the courtesan, the harlot and the lady with the pug dog. There they still sit in the rough and ready-made clothes that the male writer has had perforce to clap upon their shoulders. But Mary Carmichael" (dummying for the modern woman novelist) "will have out her scissors and fit them close to every hollow and angle. It will be a curious sight, when it comes, to see these women as they are, but we must wait a little, for Mary Carmichael will still be encumbered with that self-consciousness in the presence of 'sin' which is the legacy of our sexual barbarity. She will still wear the shoddy old fetters of class on her feet." [24] Psychologically, it is this very "self-consciousness in the presence of 'sin'" which makes Virginia Woolf speak so guardedly of Jacob's bedroom; it is this self-consciousness which causes her to cry out in "Orlando": "Let other pens treat of sex and sexuality; we quit such odious subjects as soon as we can." [25]

Yet it is on the note of sex that "Orlando" opens: "He —

[23] "Jacob's Room" p. 148.
[24] "A Room of One's Own" p. 133.
[25] "Orlando" p. 118.

for there could be no doubt of his sex, though the fashion of the time did something to disguise it —." [26] The duality of Orlando's sex embodies a doctrine congenial to Virginia Woolf. It is the theory that the great poet is a composite of man and woman, possessing the characteristic endowments of both. Such a belief would account then for the poet's intuitive understanding of both sexes; it would explain how Shakespeare could have created his women, or Jane Austen, despite her spinsterhood, create men like Mr. Bennett. It would rationalize moreover and raise at least to a plane of understanding, the recurrence of homosexuality among poets, proving that one sex had gained supremacy: in Sappho, the man, and in Shelley and Proust, the woman. But in the greatest poets, in Shakespeare and Goethe, and attempted in Orlando, both sexes have approximately equal weight. While in nature, the co-existence of these two sexes rarely takes physical form, Orlando, unhindered by natural constraint, undergoes the actual bodily changes which differentiate the sexes. Like the early magicians, he can embody his idea, acquiring the physical peculiarities of a woman when his feminine perceptions become dominant.

This theory of homosexuality among poets is not original with Virginia Woolf, though her interpretation of it is. It can be traced back, in concept, like most contemporary doctrines of abnormality, to the Greeks. In Plato's "Banquet", the Androgyns are described as a composite man-woman, whom the gods later parted. Sir Thomas Browne, whom Virginia Woolf has studied with care, writes in his "Pseudoxia Epidemica": "We must acknowledge this Androgynall condition in man" [27] while Shakespeare suggests it in the prison scene in "King Richard II":

My brain I'll prove the female to my soul:
My soul the father. [28]

Undoubtedly the most direct influence upon "Orlando" is from Coleridge, whose famous declaration: "The truth is, a great mind must be androgynous", Virginia Woolf quotes in "A Room of One's Own". [29] In his "Aids to Reflection", he accounts for the existence of good and evil in man as the co-existence of a stronger and inferior, i. e. masculine and feminine nature. The stronger male reserve embodies the will and the reason; the inferior, the unreasoning, carnal, easily tempted Eve. As a woman, Orlando has certainly this "inferior" nature; she is sensual and fallible, and her logic is more intuitive than dialectic. But as a man, Orlando's will is rather dubious, and though he philosophizes constantly, his

---

[26] "Orlando" p. 11.
[27] "Pseudodoxia Epidemica" p. 149.
[28] "King Richard II" Act V Scene V.
[29] "A Room of One's Own" p. 148.

inductions are too haphazard and subjective to be called "masculine" pellucid reason. Obviously the effeminate pole of his nature, the part most analagous to Virginia Woolf, is dominant. In "A Room of One's Own", she seeks "amateurishly to sketch a plan of the soul so that in each of us two powers preside, one male, one female; and in the man's brain the man predominates over the woman, and in the woman's brain the woman predominates over the man. The normal and comfortable state of being is that when the two live in harmony together, spiritually co-operating. If one is a man, still the woman part of the brain must have effect; and a woman also must have intercourse with the man in her. Coleridge perhaps meant this when he said that a great mind is androgynous. It is when this fusion takes place that the mind is fully fertilised and uses all its faculties." [30]

Coleridge supports this theory by the "very old tradition of the *homo androgynous*, that is, that the original man, the individual first created was bisexual", [31] a belief limited not to Greece or Egypt or Jerusalem, but found even in Persian and Indian antiquity. Orlando, explained as a conscious outgrowth of this tradition, becomes less esoteric. His change of sex appears then as a philosophic possibility, conceived in remote antiquity, rather than as the extravagance of a modern ingenious woman. Through a progression in time, he is able to embody both sexes separately. Virginia Woolf disjoins the male and female within him just as the Greek gods had disjoined the Androgyns.

There is almost no perversion in Orlando's bi-sexuality. As a man, he has a strong predilection towards women, makes violent love to princesses and lies with "loose women among treasure sacks in the holds of pirate ships." [32] His virility is certified. As a woman, she is no less attracted by men. She adopts instinctively the necessary preliminaries to love. Coquetry, modesty, and an interest in clothes become as natural as cutting off a head or committing any of the barbarisms which give the stamp to manhood. Her bearing a child proves that she is normal, if one accepts Freud's theory that perverts have renounced all claim to reproduction: „auf jede Beteiligung an der Fortpflanzung verzichtet". [33]

Orlando then remains physically true to sex, whichever it be. Turning woman, "she remembered how, as a young man, she had insisted that women must be obedient, chaste, scented and exquisitely apparalled. " 'Now I shall have to pay in my own person

---

[30] "A Room of One's Own" p. 148.
[31] "Aids To Reflection" p. 204.
[32] "Orlando" p. 137.
[33] "Einführung in die Psychoanalyse" p. 32.
[34] "Orlando" p. 133.

for those desires,' she reflected." [34] But when the Captain of the "Enamoured Lady" offers her a slice of corned beef, she is filled with the same "indescribable pleasure" which as a man she had experienced with the Russian princess. But "then she had pursued, now she fled. Which is the greater ecstasy? The man's or the woman's? And are they not perhaps the same? No, she thought, this is the most delicious (thanking the Captain but refusing), to refuse, and see him frown . . . . to resist and to yield, to yield and to resist. Surely it throws the spirit into such a rapture as nothing else can." [35]

Yet though she glories in her femininity, " 'Praise God that I'm a woman' ", [36] traces of Lesbianism appear before her conversion is complete. Through an unfinished metamorphosis, these traits are explained, for "as all Orlando's loves had been women, now through the culpable laggardry of the human frame to adapt itself to convention, though she herself was a woman, it was still a woman she loved; and if the consciousness of being of the same sex had any effect at all, it was to quicken and deepen those feelings which she had had as a man." [37] But this Lesbianism disappears, and Orlando accepts "the penalties and the privileges of her position." [38]

Regarding "Orlando" as largely autobiographical, the early period of his masculinity would be analogous to that stage in Virginia Woolf and in almost every girl, when she longs to be a boy. The freedom and experiences barred to Virginia Woolf are unquestioningly opened to him. Her feminine utopia where the woman novelist can observe every phase of life is still of the future. Even Orlando is forced to don pants, to appear at least as a man, each time she visits "Nell's parlour". It is only after a young girl has lost her curiosity and her longing for experience, that she grows reconciled to her sex and in it seeks happiness. It is at this stage that Orlando becomes a woman, returning to England in search of rest, after travelling through Turkey and encountering as many escapades as a Don Quixote or a Simplicissimus or any hero of a seventeenth century novel of adventure. Only as a man could Orlando have experienced "Life" in its variated heights and depths, in the courts of kings and in dark alleyed harbors. But it is the female Orlando, who can feel with intensity the impulse for physical and spiritual completion, for "Life and a Lover". [39] She longs not only to

[35] "Orlando" p. 132.
[36] Ibid. p. 136.
[37] Ibid. p. 137.
[38] Ibid. p. 130.
[39] Ibid. p. 156.

observe life but to feel herself part of its rhythm. She marries; she bears a son. She is physically creative, physically complete. Yet her desire to write is not obliterated. She remains a poetess, finding as much inspiration in her womanhood as before in the experiences of a man. With almost a Greek harmony of bodily and mental creativeness, she combines in herself the traits of man and woman, spiritually productive in the face of the male critics, and bodily reproductive, continuing the function of woman in the process of life.

In her attempt to understand women, Virginia Woolf seeks not only normal women, building in their femininity the pole to men, but women who combine within themselves, like the Lady Orlando, both poles, or who tend even more towards masculinity. Although her men are frequently effeminate, it is not they but the women who appear abnormal. Yet their Lesbianism is never absolutely indulged. Their Puritan upbringing and social environment make practical perversions almost inconceivable. "Chastity" Virginia Woolf writes significantly, "had then [in the seventeenth century], it has even now, a religious importance in a woman's life, and has so wrapped itself round with nerves and instincts that to cut it free and bring it to the light of day demands courage of the rarest." [40] Struggling in herself against this Puritanism, against the old social horror of sex held by respectable women, Virginia Woolf achieves a stage where she can, with objectivity, analyze sexual anomalies. To a group of college women, she makes a startling revelation:' Chloe liked Olivia . . .' Do not start. Do not blush. [Traces of her own Victorianism, suppressed at last.] Let us admit in the privacy of our own society that these things sometimes happen. Sometimes women do like women.

" 'Chloe liked Olivia,' I read. And then it struck me how immense a change was there. Chloe liked Olivia perhaps for the first time in literature. Cleopatra did not like Octavia. And how completely "Antony and Cleopatra" would have been altered had she done so! . . . . Cleopatra's only feeling about Octavia is one of jealousy. Is she taller than I am? How does she do her hair? The play, perhaps, required no more. But how interesting it would have been if the relationship between the two women had been more complicated. All these relationships between women, I thought, rapidly recalling the splendid gallery of fictitious women, are too simple." [41]

Her own conviction that as a woman she can best penetrate the consciousness of woman, has helped her to broaden her scope. In her novels, her interest in her sex begins with normal women

[40] "A Room of One's Own" p. 75.
[41] Ibid. p. 124.

and their relations to men, and matures to abnormal women and their relations to each other. The psychology of the Lesbian attracts her; she sees in it that duality of sex, that coexistence of man and woman, which she describes at length in "A Room of One's Own" and substantiates in "Orlando". In Mrs. Dalloway's relation to Sally Seton lie definite masculine traits; Clarissa is charmed by Sally's voice and her recklessness; she has the man's instinct to protect the woman he loves. The feeling "was protective on her side, sprang from a sense of being in league together, a presentiment of something that was was bound to part them (they spoke of marriage always as a catastrophe), which led to this chivalry, this protective feeling . . ." [42] A dread of marriage, the hallucination of man as a brute occurs so frequently in a girl's adolescence that it may well be regarded as normal. It is the Brünhilde instinct for self-preservation; the virginal fear of losing her identity and strength. Yet Clarissa's revulsion from men continues long after her marriage. As a girl, though she gives it no visible expression, this dread finds strong outlet in her emotions. She recoils from the thought that Sally whom she loves, is to be broken by men: "she felt only how Sally was being mauled already, maltreated." [43] The masculinity of her nature, her search for that sensation from women which normally men experience, is most apparent when Sally has "kissed her on the lips." "The most exquisite moment of her whole life . . . . The whole world might have turned upside down! The others disappeared; there she was alone with Sally." [44] Such androgynal sensations are forced to remain concealed, for she "had a scruple picked up Heaven knows where", her social bans, "or, as she felt, sent by Nature (who is invariably wise)." [45] It is an instinctive or acquired purity, thoroughly understood by Virginia Woolf. Thus, though Mrs. Dalloway reproaches herself for it, in her relations to her husband, she is involuntarily frigid. "She could not dispel a virginity which clung to her like a sheet. Lovely in girlhood, suddenly there came a moment — for example on the river beneath the woods at Clieveden — when, through some contraction of this cold spirit, she had failed him. And then at Constantinople, and again and again." [46] Frigidity assumes towards her husband the warmth she had experienced towards Sally. She analyzes this neurosis: "She could see what she lacked. It was not beauty; it was not mind. It was something central

---

[42] "Mrs. Dalloway" p. 47.
[43] Ibid. p. 50.
[44] Ibid. p. 49.
[45] Ibid. p. 44.
[46] Ibid. p. 44.

which permeated, something warm which broke up surfaces and rippled the cold contact of man and woman, or of women together. For *that* she could dimly perceive." [47] "That" italicized, this homosexual abnormality, Virginia Woolf recoils from naming. Like a priest raising his voice with disdain, she brands it with italics and then describes less cryptically how Mrs. Dalloway "could not resist yielding to the charm of a woman, not a girl, of a woman confessing, as to her they often did, some scrape, some folly. And whether it was pity, or their beauty, or that she was older, or some accident — like a faint scent, or a violin next door (so strange is the power of sounds at certain moments)" suggesting the fetichisms and poetic sensibilities so often inherent in Lesbianism, "she did undoubtedly then feel what men felt. Only for a moment; but it was enough. It was a sudden revelation, a tinge like a blush which one tried to check and then, as it spread, one yielded to its expansion, and rushed to the farthest verge and there quivered and felt the world come closer, swollen with some astonishing significance, some pressure of rapture, which split its thin skin and gushed and poured with an extraordinary alleviation over the cracks and sores! Then, for that moment, she had seen an illumination; a match burning in a crocus; an inner meaning almost expressed. But the close withdrew; the hard softened. It was over — the moment." [48] In its flowing sensuality, this experience recalls the ecstatic moments which D. H. Lawrence perceives between man and woman. The same sensation of heightened living is in both, the sense of touching the core of life. "The pressure of rapture", the moment of spiritual conjugation between two women has the surging rhythm of Lawrence's "whirlpools of sensation swirling deeper through all her tissue and consciousness, till she was one perfect concentric fluid of feeling." [49]

"But this question of love," Mrs. Dalloway meditates, "this falling in love with women. Take Sally Seton; her relation in the old days with Sally Seton. Had not that, after all been love?" [50] Here is little attempt at concealment. Clarissa's abnormality, however much poeticized, seems indisputable. All social attempts to deny it, her marriage, her maternity, are useless. She is inhibited by the rigidity of her education; "she knew nothing about sex nothing about social problems." [51] Problems evidently of perversions as well as wealth. "She had once seen an

[47] "Mrs. Dalloway" p. 44.
[48] Ibid. p. 44.
[49] "Lady Chatterley's Lover" p. 158.
[50] "Mrs. Dalloway" p. 45.
[51] Ibid. p. 46.

old man who had dropped dead in a field" her only knowledge
of the nude male body; "she had seen cows just after their calves
were born. But Aunt Helena never liked discussion of anything
(when Sally gave her William Morris, it had to be wrapped in
brown paper)." [52] To break completely from such an
environment would necessitate more strength and perhaps a
deeper, more dramatic neurosis than Clarissa's. She does nothing
to shock society or Aunt Helena; she does nothing to violate her
own sense of purity. Towards her husband, she appears as the
Victorian martyr-wife, surrendering to him her passionless love.
But she represents a new understanding of this Victorianism;
Virginia Woolf, with the aid of Freud and modern sex-conscious-
ness, throws a romantic light upon this concept of inviolable
virginity.

The relation between Elizabeth, Mrs. Dalloway's daughter,
and her governess, Miss Kilman, is another example of Virginia
Woolf's feminine interest in the contact between two women. The
disparity in age, however, makes this relationship seem less
psychotic than that between Clarissa and Sally, in love with each
other's beauty or protective strength. Here the attraction is that
of teacher and pupil, of admiration for superior intelligence, and
in the governess, of a diverted instinct of maternity. It is a
psychologic reflection of the relationships so universal in
girl's schools that they are now almost naturally accepted.
Frequently known under the expressive name of "crush", they are
indicative probably of the physical desire. As with Clarissa, Miss
Kilman's relationship takes no form obnoxious to society, but the
emotions and the conscious sensations which society condemns,
are present. Miss Kilman, an unhappy character, forced, by
her inability to attract men, into almost a state of sexlessness,
diverts all her emotions to Elizabeth. With the peculiar
androgynousness of an Orlando or a Mrs. Dalloway, she experiences an overwhelming desire to possess Elizabeth. "If she could
grasp her, if she could clasp her, if she could make her hers
absolutely and for ever and then die; that was all she wanted." [53]
Her need is as great as a man's, her jealousy seems even greater;
she "could not let her go! this youth, that was so beautiful; this
girl, whom she genuinely loved." [54] She is painfully aware of
her desire, and with the tragic apprehension that it is doomed,
she frustrates it helplessly herself. She feels a compulsion to
reveal herself to Elizabeth in all her spiritual ugliness, in her
egotism, her intelligence and her ostentatious poverty.

[52] "Mrs. Dalloway" p. 46.
[53] Ibid. p. 183.
[54] Ibid. p. 182.

Elizabeth's attitude is less androgynous. She is fascinated by the older woman, but her attraction is mystic, not sensual. Her religious appetencies have been aroused. She is edified by a quest for God just as Mrs. Dalloway is for beauty. She loses herself, like countless women, in apocryphal revelations, in "religious ecstasy". [55] Miss Kilman, initiating her into Communion, supplying her with books, becomes an admirable medium, dispensable as soon as Elizabeth outgrows her need.

Each of these women represents a different phase of the contemporary feminine problem, of the psychopathic women who are only now finding understanding. Recent works like Radclyffe Hall's "The Well of Loneliness" published in 1928, have brought new sympathy for the Sapphic relationships of women.

Devoid of beauty or womanly charm, Miss Kilman represents that mass of intellectual women unable to attain normal happiness. She compensates by becoming a blue-stocking and a religious fanatic. She develops her mind and her spirit, because her body is negative, and through her mind she seeks to attract others. Discouraged by men, she turns to women, especially to those who possess the feminine charm she lacks. She is not a Lesbian, not more masculine than feminine, but a woman forced by circumstances, by her physical heritage for which she is hardly to blame, to divert her impulses. Envy and jealousy take the place of love. She seeks in Elizabeth her lost youth, and beholds in her what she herself would have longed to be. Elizabeth, contrastively, represents the problem of the adolescent girl, seeking some spiritual outlet. Her attachment to the older woman arouses a jealousy and hatred in Clarissa, her mother, generating a further complexity in this structure of woman relationships.

Almost of necessity, Virginia Woolf's women are far more psychologically presented than are her men. Just as self-analysis generally precedes an understandig of mankind, so women novelists have usually first to analyze and comprehend women before they can turn to men. Virginia Woolf is still too novitiate; she understands women with subtle variations, but she falls short in her analysis of men. Almost all are of the upper middle class; her milieu is not that of the Zoloesque servants or D. H. Lawrence gamekeepers. The great majority of her men are poets, like Jacob or Bernard, and as poets, she can justify their effeminate traits. She can infuse in them her comprehension of the poetic personality analyzed within herself. But her politicians, husbands or rejected lovers lack the complexity and the greatness of conception which she

---

[55] "Mrs. Dalloway" p. 16.

attempts in her women. The flaccidity of a character like Hugh Whitbread, a friend of Mrs. Dalloway's, is as denotative of Virginia Woolf's observations of men as of her ability to make them real. His personality is superficial and shallow. He has reached his perfection in his slightly absurd position of royal shoe-shiner. Having acquired the protective shell of the perfect gentleman, he is utterly sterile within. All propensities for psychic interest are lacking; the mother-son Oedipus complex which would perhaps correlate in a study of man the Lesbianism which Virginia Woolf analyzes in women, becomes simply the unselfishness with which an English gentleman escorts his mother on his holidays. Thus "when his old mother wanted him to give up shooting or to take her to Bath he did it without a word." [56] The situation presents the potentialities for depth, but Hugh, typical of the class he represents, remains with "no heart, no brain", [57] courteous to women and self-satisfied.

In her desire to create heroic women, Virginia Woolf frequently makes her men, in contrast, a negating force, a sterile element. In the conflict of man and woman, she reflects her ever-present problem of the struggle between the critic and the poet. Unlike most male poets, she conceives woman as the creative power in life and man as its destroyer. Where Mrs. Ramsay of "To the Lighthouse" is the great mother, the symbol of fertility, her husband suffers from feminine prejudice in Virginia Woolf. Mrs. Ramsay seemed "to pour erect into the air a rain of energy, a column of spray, looking at the same time animated and alive as if all her energies were being fused into force, burning and illuminating (quietly though she sat, taking up her stocking again), and into this delicious fecundity, this fountain and spray of life, the fatal sterility of the male plunged itself, like a beak of brass, barren and bare. He wanted sympathy. He was a failure, he said . . . . It was sympathy he wanted, to be assured of his genius, first of all, and then to be taken within the circle of life, warmed and soothed, to have his senses restored to him, his barrenness made fertile, and all the rooms of the house made full of life — the drawing-room; behind the drawing-room the kitchen; above the kitchen the bedrooms; and beyond them the nurseries; they must be furnished, they must be filled with life." [58]

Woman is for her the genius of life. It is she who creates and satisfies the human need for a room, for a setting of rested

[56] "Mrs. Dalloway" p. 10.
[57] Ibid. p. 10.
[58] "To the Lighthouse" p. 62.

fulfilment. All the incongruent shapes in the room, its people, its chairs, its reflecting mirrors, are given significance and design by the presence of a woman: "the whole of the effort of merging and flowing and creating rested on her." [59] With true artistry, Virginia Woolf attempts to make of such women, figures of completion. She does not infuse them, like a social moralist, with ideals for converting mankind. The more masculine need to educate the world fails her. Where she can describe the haphazard irrationalities of their lives, of life itself, she is most successful. " 'Je n'enseigne poinct; je raconte.' " [60] she quotes significantly from Montaigne. Her novels are thus freed from all desire to lay down a code of morals for the world. Ethics and determinism have given way to pure toleration. " 'I am very tolerant,' " says Bernard. " 'I am not a moralist. I have too great a sense of the shortness of life and its temptations to rule red lines' ". [61] The innately lawless woman is discernible; oppressed herself by the codes of man-made ethics, Virginia Woolf can understand evil without desiring to reform it. In her novels, she seeks not to condemn or ameliorate the world, but to remirror life, poetically, without pedantism. Like her own observation of Jane Austen, "She would not move one brick or blade of grass in a world which provides her with such exquisite delight." [62]

Thus she satirizes the world reformers: the politicians, suffragists, blue stockings, and even social workers. She has as little taste for active politics as for active militarism; she is determined to leave them to others, preferably to men. The tremendous sacrifices which women make in their determination to reform the world, she describes negatingly in "Night and Day". Mary, with all the propensities for a life of love and motherhood withers into an emancipating old maid with day dreams of the man she might have married. She goes to ruin because she has lost her femininity in liberating womanhood. Almost certainly inspired by the Mary of "Pride and Prejudice", she has the same faults, the terseness, the partial subversion of her femininity which Jane Austen gives her heroine, with the great exception that the nineteenth century woman, through reawakening womanhood, saves herself from spinsterhood. "It is sometimes a disadvantage to be so very guarded," philosophizes Jane Austen, warning women against the danger of suppressing their womanly emotions. "If a woman conceals her affection with

---

[59] Ibid. p. 131.
[60] "The Common Reader" p. 93.
[61] "The Waves" p. 237.
[62] "The Common Reader" p. 200.

the same skill from the object of it, she may lose the opportunity of fixing him," the opportunity of completing herself, "and it will be but poor consolation to believe the world equally in the dark." [63] Diverted by political socialism, Mary's development is hampered, and her affections unnaturally suppressed. She has sacrificed those mysterious charms with which Virginia Woolf endows her heroines, her women who are loved. Unbroken by life, they are the women who cling to their femininity, who live it rather than subvert it into propaganda. They are the great mothers like Mrs. Ramsay, or Mrs. Ambrose of "The Voyage Out", the women bound to earth and symbolizing in themselves earth's process. It is they, the women who stand in the room, who diffuse it with a life contingent upon their own, who are Virginia Woolf's ideals, her great characters. Not the women who flee, who rebel or protest or dream at the window, but those who infuse the room with intellectual life through their deep understanding, and physical life through bearing children. Although she understands the strugglers and revolters, she revels in the women who are no longer distorted by a warrior attitude; the women who have "consumed all impediments and become incandescent." [64]

An ideal of perfection is created in these characters. That completion which Virginia Woolf had sought in her spiritual mothers, is in her women, fulfilled. A Greek perfection marks them; they are at once intellectual and sensual, balancing androgynously, as in "Orlando", the creativeness of men and of maternal women. Physically submitting to the laws of life, of reproduction, they stand also beyond these laws, mentally productive.

Their tremendous experiences of motherhood and love, Virginia Woolf pierces with self-analytic understanding. She idealizes, though she herself lacks, the rhythmic experiences of bearing children. Her women have the reality of the details and irrelevancies of life. The powerfulness with which a man heaves tremendous figures out of his own imagination; the formal strength which converts a lyric Shakespeare into a dramatic realist, fails her. Seen through her women, her writing reflects the order of life rather than the static finality of a closed drama. She is poetically idyllic, bound by her intellect to earth.

Where she seeks for her novels the perfected woman rather than the revolter, she is, in her essays and her personal strivings, a struggler herself. She continues the revolt of women. She is a spiritual suffragist. With a strong faith in progress, in evolution,

---

[63] "Pride and Prejudice" p. 158.
[64] "A Room of One's Own" p. 88.

she places herself in the struggle for independence, the struggle which had broken Margaret of Newcastle, which had obstructed Charlotte Brontë, and obscured the writings of the women of the past. She saves her own art from becoming the organ of her struggle by presenting her ideal of womanhood as a completed fact. She retains her serenity, conscious however that the struggle is by no means ended, that women are still not free. She represents a deeper, evolved phase in the movement of feminine emancipation. The cry for independence which the women of the nineteenth century had sounded, she intensifies and normalizes. The violence and fanaticism which had driven the early suffragists, like Mrs. Pankhurst, to sacrifice their innate femininity, in her, loses its extravagance. She seeks to show her equality with man, not through adopting masculine neck-ties or cigars but through maintaining her femininity, and in it, in its very polarity with man, manifesting her equal heights. She desires not to imitate men nor to lose herself on their grounds; hers is the more organic struggle of opposite though equal forces.

She identifies herself with the women who are still forced to protest, blaming their struggle upon a masculine hierarchy. With optimism, she calls out to other women to struggle with her, to perfect themselves in laying the road for the greater women to come. She is not disillusioned, not the futilitarian which Harold Nicolson and the contemporary critics would make her. Far more, she is a pioneer, with all the self-sacrificing requisites which an ideal demands. She is working not only to penetrate her own depths, but to lay the way for the great poetess of the future "to walk among us in the flesh. This opportunity . . . . is now coming within your power to give her. For my belief is that if we live another century or so — I am talking of the common life which is the real life and not of the little separate lives which we live as individuals — and have five hundred a year each of us and rooms of our own; if we have the habit of freedom and the courage to write exactly what we think; . . . . then the opportunity will come and the dead poet who was Shakespeare's sister will put on the body which she so often laid down. Drawing her life from the lives of the unknown who were her forerunners, as her brother did before her, she will be born. As for her coming without that preparation, without that effort on our part, without that determination that when she is born again she shall find it possible to live and write her poetry, that we cannot expect, for that would be impossible. But I maintain that she would come if we worked for her, and that so to work, even in poverty and obscurity, is worth while." [65]

[65] "A Room of One's Own" p. 172.

The tremendous battle-cry for spiritual freedom, for the breaking of chains, which had characterized men like Shelley, is sounded now by women. Just as Nietzsche had proclaimed the Men of the future, so Virginia Woolf and her contemporaries, women like Rebecca West and Dorothy Richardson, are making the way for the Women of the future. The political emancipation is one step; the intellectual emancipation must follow. The woman of the hearth becomes a woman standing in the tumult of life, defending herself. Her old bondage to her father and brothers and sons is struggling for release. She has found the will to rise up from slavery just as men have risen up from slavery, nordics as well as American negroes. Her frailty is a myth, no less forgiveable than the frailty which makes men petty thieves. In her old state of slavery, she was a kind of petty thief, forced because she was hungry, to steal learning from books she hid or from worldly experiences, for whose sin she was hanged or condemned. She was denied what in a man was taken for granted or humorously tolerated: his ambitions, his curiosities, his wild oats. The material for observation has failed her. It is when she has gone out and experienced, as men are permitted to experience in the world, that she may create as Shakespeare did. It is when she has perfected and combined her physical life with her spiritual that she can become a great artist.

The woman of the past found an intimation of the laws of nature, of life and imortality, in bearing children; the woman of the future, retaining this experience, will give it words and form. Virginia Woolf, of the present, is still a seeker, struggling to prepare the world for a woman Shakespeare, a woman Rembrandt, even a woman Christ. She is a transitional link between the past which produced a Jane Austen and the future yet to produce the great "Shakespearianna". Conscious of her limitations, she finds a beautiful gratification in being one of Her mediators, one of the spiritual mothers.

The woman she is helping to create will culminate in herself the physical creativeness of the past with the mental creativeness of women like Virginia Woolf — the woman of today.

BIBLIOGRAPHY

Of Virginia Woolf's Writings:

"The Voyage Out", London, Hogarth Press, 1929 first pub. 1915.
"Night and Day", London, Hogarth Press, 1930 first pub. 1919.
"Jacob's Room", London, Hogarth Press, 1929 first pub. 1922.
"Mr. Bennett and Mrs. Brown", New York, Doubleday, Doran, 1928 first pub. 1924.
"Mrs. Dalloway", Leipzig, Tauchnitz, 1929 first pub. 1925.
"The Common Reader", New York, Harcourt, Brace, 1925.
"To the Lighthouse", London, Hogarth Press, 1929 first publ. 1927.
"Orlando", Leipzig, Tauchnitz, 1929 first pub. 1928.
"A Room of One's Own", London, Hogarth Press, 1931 first pub. 1929.
"The Waves", London, Hogarth Press, 1931.

Of Virginia Woolf's Influences:

Austen, Jane: "Pride and Prejudice". Oxford, Clarendon Press, 1919.

Bergson, Henri: "L'Energie Spirituelle, Essais et Conferences". Paris F. Alcan 1920, 6th ed.

Browne, Sir Thomas: "Works". ed. by Charles Sayle, Edinburgh, John Grant, 1927.

Burke, Edmund: "Writings and Speeches". Oxford University Press, 1907.

Coleridge, Samuel: "Aids to Reflection". London, William Pickering, 1848.

De Quincey, Thomas: "The Confessions of an Opium-Eater and Other Essays". London, Macmillan, 1924.

Einstein, Albert: „Vier Vorlesungen über Relativitätstheorie". held in May, 1921 at Princeton University, Braunschweig 1922.

Eliot, T. S.: "The Lovesong of J. Alfred Prufrock" in "An Anthology of American Poetry". New York, The Modern Library, 1929.

Fielding, Henry: "The History of Tom Jones, a Foundling", ed. by George Saintsbury, London, Dent, 1910.

Freud, Sigmund: „Vorlesungen zur Einführung in die Psychoanalyse". Wien, Internationaler Psychoanalytischer Verlag, 1930, Kleinoktav-Ausgabe.

Gibbon, Edward: "The Decline and Fall of the Roman Empire". Oxford University Press, 1914.

Greene, Robert: "The History of Orlando Furioso". London, Routledge, Warne, and Routledge, 1861.

Joyce, James: "Ulysses". Paris, Shakespeare, 1926.

Lawrence, D. H.: "Lady Chatterley's Lover". Florence, privately printed, 1929.

Milton, John: "Poetical Works", ed. by William Aldis Wright, Cambridge University Press, 1903.

Proust, Marcel: "A la Recherche du Temps Perdu". Paris, Librairie
 Gallimard, 1920.
Wordsworth, William: "Wordsworth's Literary Criticism", ed. by Nowell
 C. Shmith, London, Oxford Univ. Press, 1925.

Of Virginia Woolf's Critics:

Badenhausen, Ingeborg: „Die Sprache Virginia Woolfs". Marburg 1932,
 a doctorate dissertation limited almost solely to the accidents of
 grammar.
Fehr, Bernhard: „Englische Prosa von 1880 bis zur Gegenwart". Leipzig,
 Tauchnitz, 1927.
Forster, E. M.: "Aspects of the Novel". New York, Harcourt, Brace, 1927.
Manly and Rickert: "Contemporary British Literature". London, Harrap, 1929.
Muir, Edwin: "The Structure of the Novel". London, L. and V. Woolf, 1928.
Nicolson, Harold: "The New Spirit in Literature". London, The British
 Broadcasting Corporation, 1931.

A MYSTERY SOLVED

A MYSTERY SOLVED

How 28 Volumes of Virginia Woolf's Diaries and More Than 100 of Her Letters Left London and Landed in the Berg Collection of the 5th Avenue New York City Public Library

I owe this book to an epiphany.

On June 15, 2004, Doris Schechter, whom I had brought from Italy to New York in 1944 as an enchanting five-year old, with a thousand other World War II refugees, sat next to me in Carnegie Hall.

We were listening to a recital by two gifted teachers from SUNY Oswego, when Doris leaned over and whispered in my ear, "I just had an epiphany. Why don't you get your publishers to republish your doctoral thesis on Virginia Woolf? It could be a fundraiser for some of the causes you're involved with."

Excited by the idea, I took Doris's epiphany to my editor, Philip Turner, at Carroll and Graf. The idea percolated. A few weeks later, the three letters from Virginia Woolf turned up.

Philip called me. "Drop everything you're doing. We're going to do it. We're going to reprint your whole dissertation with the three letters. We want you to write an introduction telling how you wrote the first feminist interpretation of Virginia Woolf. Make it as personal as you can. You have to do it fast. We want to bring it out in the spring of 2005."

I was working on volume 3 of my memoirs, tentatively called *In Spite of Time: How to Live at 93*. I put it aside, and worked seven days a week, writing "My Hours with Virginia Woolf." It gave me the joy of leafing through many of Virginia Woolf's books and essays and Leonard Woolf's masterful autobiography, *Downhill All the Way*.

While writing the introduction, I wondered how twenty-eight volumes of Virginia Woolf's diaries and hundreds of her letters and original manuscripts had come from London to the Berg Collection in New York City's 5th Avenue Library.

I have two brilliant surrogate daughters; one, Doris Schechter, who had the epiphany, is now a creative restaurant owner and author of a handsome cookbook, named for her restaurant, My Most Favorite Dessert. The second surrogate daughter, Patti Kenner, is a social activist, philanthropist, and fundraiser who, with her 92-year-old father, runs Campus Coach Lines. One day, answering Patti's question on the phone, "What are you up to now?," I told her I wanted to find out how Virginia Woolf's diaries and letters came to the New York Public Library.

Patti, who knows most of the movers and shakers in New York, said "I'll call you back in a few minutes."

Five minutes later, she was on the line again. "I called my friend, Dr. Paul Le Clerc, the president and chief executive officer of the New York Public Library. He's handling it."

I had hardly hung up when the phone rang again. "This is Isaac Gerwirtz. I'm the curator of the Berg Collection. How may I help you?"

"I'm looking for an answer: How did Virginia Woolf's diaries and letters come into a collection named for two Jewish doctors?"

He suggested I come to the library, and within an hour I was at the Berg Collection where Isaac, efficient and eager to help, assured me that he would get me the answer. "It will take some time," he said, "but we will have it."

I thanked him.

"I have to rush out now," he spoke quickly, "but my people here will bring you whatever you need. I will be back in a little while. You can stay as late as you want, even eight o'clock, if you need to."

I was alone now with Virginia Woolf, once again reading her diaries, and once again finding the strange things she had written about me. Isaac returned, and when I stood up to leave and thank him for his help, he presented me with a slim red volume called *Brothers: The Origins of the Henry W. and Albert A. Berg Collection of English and American Literature, The New York Public Library*.

Written by the former curator, Lola L. Szladits, it told the story of these two distinguished American Jewish physicians, who created the Berg Collection. In Vienna, their father, Moritz Berg, had dreamed of becoming a physician but could never afford medical school. So in 1862, while the Civil War raged in America, he and his wife, Josephine Schiff, gathered up their first-born son, Henry, and sailed in steerage to a country at war.

Like many penniless immigrants, Moritz gave up his dream, forsaking medicine and becoming a tailor. He fathered seven more children. Henry, the oldest, and Albert, the youngest, fulfilled their father's dream, becoming doctors, educated at City College and then Columbia's College for Physicians and Surgeons. They soon were on the staff of Mount Sinai Hospital, and when Moritz died of cancer, they became specialists in cancer treatment.

Medicine was part of their lives, buying real estate was another. Bachelors, they lived together in a townhouse they owned on East 73rd Street, and amassed a fortune of over $8,000,000. They used that money to purchase rare books and manuscripts, and spread their fortune among a bevy of Jewish and non-Jewish hospitals, libraries, universities, and high schools, also donating two million dollars to the New York Public Library. Henry had already died when Albert A. Berg opened the Berg Collection in Henry's memory with a moving speech on October 11, 1940:

> *These books, manuscripts, and letters, together with the appointments in this room, were the dear friends of my late brother and myself. In presenting them to you and the Trustees of the Public Library of our City, and through you to the public it is with the pleasant anticipation that their new friends will use them and love them as much as we did.*

The book about the brothers made no mention of Virginia Woolf's writings. But an e-mail arrived from Isaac Gewirtz on October 29, 2004:

> *Dear Dr. Gruber,*
> *The history of the Berg's acquisition of its Virginia Woolf papers is considerably more complex than I suspected or than has been reported. I've spent several hours examining the voluminous correspon-*

dence and memos from that period and summarize my findings for you, below. . . .

Twenty-eight bound volumes of Virginia Woolf's diaries for the period January 1, 1915–March 24, 1941, as well as virtually all of Virginia Woolf's papers were sold by Leonard Woolf to the rare book and manuscript dealer Hamill and Barker (Chicago) in the spring of 1957, under the stipulations that they should not be resold until after his death, and that the purchaser must be a public or university library.

Later, in 1957, the Berg, in person of Dr. John Gordan, the Berg's first Curator, entered into negotiations with Hamill & Barker for the papers' purchase: novels, short stories, essays, correspondence (incoming and any copies of her outgoing), and diaries. . . . Only a few significant manuscripts were absent from the transaction, most notably The Voyage Out *(which was in the Bodleian),* Night and Day, Orlando, *and* A Room of One's Own. *In 1962, Leonard Woolf donated to the Berg a part of the original manuscript of* The Voyage Out. *In the early 1960s, the Berg purchased* Night and Day *and* A Room of One's Own, *as well as* Notes on Books *and a 50-page portion of the original draft and the various versions, in typescript, of* Between the Acts, *from H&B. . . . Though Woolf did not object to the Berg's purchase of the diaries with the rest of the papers, he insisted that the diaries not be delivered to the Berg until after his death, though Gordan had explained to H&B (who communicated this to Woolf) that Library policy forbade paying for material prior to receiving it. The Library and H&B surmounted this obstacle by stating in the purchase agreement that H&B would deliver all of the papers specified except for the diaries, that the Berg would pay for the papers delivered, and that the diaries would be delivered and paid for after Mr. Woolf's death.*

In 1964, the Berg purchased from H&B two slim diaries for 1905 and for the Sept. 7–Oct. 1, 1919, which are not part of the 28-volume series. In 1968, the Berg purchased from H&B The Years; *ca. 120 letters to Leonard Woolf; and 5 letters to Virginia Woolf. In 1980, we purchased two autograph and five typed undated letters [1928–1932] to Nancy Pearn, and in 1993, a typed letter to Quentin Bell.*

This summarizes the acquisition history of the great bulk of our Virginia Woolf papers, but it is a story that should probably be told someday in greater detail. If I ever find the time, I will attempt to do so. For now, I hope that the information I've provided will suit your needs. It has been a delight working with you and I hope that we will soon have the opportunity to renew our acquaintance.

With best wishes,
Isaac Gewirtz

I owe Isaac Gewirtz my deepest gratitude. His detective work had answered the question of how Virginia Woolf's diaries and letters crossed the Atlantic and were now safely guarded and cherished in the oak-paneled walls of the Berg Collection.

There are numerous other people to whom I owe thanks in writing this book. Foremost is my editor, Philip Turner, whose enthusiasm and advice have been equaled only by his constant but well-meaning pressure urging me to meet my deadline. My agent, Michael Carlisle, was equally enthusiastic and helpful. Much gratitude goes to my assistants, especially Liesl Yamaguchi, who was a joy to work with, efficient and disciplined, a straight-A sophomore at Columbia University, who divided her time between classes and taking dictation from me, typing as fast as I talked; Maressa Gershowitz, my research assistant and archivist, who found the VW letters and who raced through my filing cabinets, each time finding exactly what I was looking for; and Leah Krauss, a Barnard College freshman who, like Liesl, could type as fast as I talked, and who was willing to run back and forth between Barnard and my apartment to work on the Introduction often five hours at a time.

I am grateful to my niece Dava Sobel, the gifted author of *Longitude* and *Galileo's Daughter*; to my good friend Heidi Stella, junior dean at Oxford University; to my good friend Barbara Ribakove-Gordon, a professional editor and writer with whom I made two trips to Ethiopia to help in the rescue of Ethiopian Jews; to Dan Levin, novelist, biographer, poet, and teacher at CW Post, whom I first met during World War II when he was a marine correspondent; to his son Forrest Levin, a teacher of math at the college level and a wiz at helping me with my computer; to my step-daughter Barbara Seaman, the feminist health expert, who spent forty years in the wilderness decrying the indiscriminate use of hormones; to the members of the Writers Workshop, especially Gerald Jonas, who writes the science fiction column for the *New York Times Book Review* and whose critiques are always on target; to my good friends Dr. David Peretz and Dr. Robert Naiman, who helped me understand some of the symptoms of bipolar disorder, and that one of its symptoms is to end the pain by committing suicide; Dr. Alice Ginott Cohn, a psychologist and loyal friend.

Of course, I cannot fail to mention Virginia Woolf herself, nor her graciousness in the three letters to me and the magical twilight I spent with her and her husband Leonard as she lay in front of the fireplace at 52 Tavistock Square.

INDEX

A

activity vs. passivity, 107-108
Aids to Reflection (Coleridge), 146, 147
androgyny, 146–148, 148–149
anti-Semitism. *see also* Nazi Germany
   of Virginia Woolf, 35
Aristotelian unities, 111–113
art, significance of, 122–123
Austen, Jane, 63, 64, 66, 138–139
   Pride and Prejudice, 155–156
authors, male, influence of, 88–89

B

Balderston, John Lloyd, *Berkeley
   Square*, 114
Barnes & Noble, 40
Bell, Julian, 30
Berg, Albert, 165
Berg Collection, New York Public
   Library, 25, 29–30, 164-167
    origins of, 164–166
    acquisition of Woolf papers, 165–167
Berg, Moritz, 165
Bergson, Henri, 109–111
Berkeley Square (Balderston), 114
"Biographical Sketch of Dr. Ruth
   Gruber" (promotional pamphlet),
   48–51
bipolar disorder, 9, 10, 34–35, 35–36, 168
Bolsher, Peggy, 14–15, 39
Bronte, Charlotte, *Jane Eyre*, 67
Bronte, Emily, 64
*Brothers: The Origins of the Henry W
   and Albert A. Berg Collection of
   English and American Literature, The
   New York Public Library* (Szladits),

164–165
Browne, Sir Thomas, *Pseudoxia
   Epidemica*, 146
   Urn Burial, 90–91
Burke, Edmund, *Speech on the Nabob of
   Arcot's Debts*, 86–87

C

Carroll and Graf Publishers, 163
citation of works, in Woolf, 84–87, 91–92
   incorporation of, 87–88
classicism
   flaws of, 128
   vs. romanticism, 125–129
clothing, symbolism of, 140–141
Cohn, Alice Ginott, 168
Coleridge, Samuel, *Aids to Reflection*,
   146, 147
Common Reader, The, 85, 92, 155
*Connecticut Yankee in King Arthur's
   Court* (Twain), 114
consciousness, stream of, 107–108, 111
Cornish, George, 8, 22
correspondence
   Barnes and Noble, letter of refer-
    ence, 40
   Isaac Gewirtz to Ruth Gruber, 165–167
   Margaret West to Ruth Gruber, 23–24
    reproduction of document, 42
   Nigel Nicolson to Ruth Gruber, 31–32
    reproduction of documents, 52, 54
   P. Bolsher to Ruth Gruber, 14–15
    reproduction of document, 39
   Ruth Gruber to Margaret West, 24
    reproduction of document, 43
   Ruth Gruber to Nigel Nicolson, 53

Ruth Gruber to Virginia Woolf, 23, 32–33
   reproduction of documents, 41, 45, 46
Virginia Woolf to Ethel Smyth, 35
Virginia Woolf to Julian Bell, 30
Virginia Woolf to Leonard Woolf, 35–36
Virginia Woolf to Ruth Gruber, 26–27, 29, 33–34
   reproduction of documents, 44, 45, 47
creativity, of women, 154–155, 156
critics
   denouncing, 62–63, 92
   power of, 61–62, 64
   satire of, 78–79

D

day, single, symbolism of, 130–131
De Quincey, Thomas, *Dream-Fugue*, 91, 93, 95
Decline and Fall of the Roman Empire (Gibbon), 85
diaries, of Virginia Woolf, 25–26, 31, 32, 34
Dostoevsky, Fyodor, *Stavrogin's Confession*, 86
Downhill All the Way (L. Woolf), 34
Dream-Fugue (De Quincey), 91, 93, 95
dreams and illusions, 105
dress, symbolism of, 140–141
duality, 124–139

E

egotism vs. integrity, 65
Einfuhrung in die Psychoanalyse (Freud), 147
Einstein, Albert, 9
   Relativitatstheorie, 114–115
Eliot, T. S., 2–3
   The Lovesong of J. Alfred Prufrock, 88
emotionalism vs. realism, 106
Ethiopian refugees, 168
Euphues and his England (Lyly), 90

F

femininity, 67–68
   expression in literature, 138
feminism, 155–158. *see also* sexism
   Woolf's influence on, 9
Feuchtwanger, Lion, *The Oppermanns*, 9
Fielding, Henry, 62
food, descriptions of, 141–142
formalism, 141–142
Freud, Sigmund, *Einfuhrung in die Psychoanalyse*, 147
Fry, Roger, 2

G

Gabriel, Hugo, 13, 22
Galileo's Daughter (Sobel), 167
gender changes, in *Orlando*, 93, 94
genius, 115–116
genius, quality of, 115–116
Georgian writers, 97
Gershowitz, Marissa, 1, 167
Gewirtz, Isaac, 164, 165–167
Gibbon, Edward, *Decline and Fall of the Roman Empire*, 84–85
Goering, Hermann, 4
Gordan, John, 166
Greene, Robert, *The History of Orlando Furioso*, 78
Gruber, Ruth
   academic career, 10–15, 10–16
     in Europe, 12–18
     obtains Ph.D, 17–19, 20–22
   "Biographical Sketch" (promotional pamphlet), 48–51
   dissertation published by Tauchnitz Press, 22–25
   early career, 22–23
   I Went to the Soviet Arctic, 8
   media coverage, 20–22
   meets Virginia Woolf, 1–3
   writes dissertation on Woolf, 13–15
     defends thesis, 16–17

H

Hall, Radclyffe, *The Well of Loneliness*, 153

INDEX

Halls, Catherine, 31

Hamburg-Amerika cruise line, 20

Hamill and Barker (manuscript dealers), 166

Herz family, 28–29

History of Orlando Furioso (Greene), 78

Hitler, Adolf, 3–5, 7, 8, 16

Hogarth Press, 14, 35

homosexuality, 146, 148, 149–152

hope, and nihilism, 117–120

The Hours (film), 2

I

I Went to the Soviet Arctic (Gruber), 8

identity, struggle for, 125

illusions and dreams, 105

Institute of International Education (IIE), 11

integrity, concept of, 63, 64–65
   compromise of, 76
   vs. egotism, 65

intuition vs. rationalism, 109–111

Israel, 8

J

Jacob's Room (Woolf), 88, 97–103, 120, 141, 144–145

Jane Eyre (Bronte), 67

Jewish refugees, 8–9, 20, 22, 28, 163, 168

Jonas, Gerald, 168

Joyce, James, 89, 93
   Ulysses, 91, 95–96

K

Kenner, Patti, 164

Keynes, John Maynard, 2

Kidman, Nicole, 2

King Richard III (Shakespeare), 146

Krauss, Leah, 167

L

Lady Chatterley's Lover (Lawrence), 94, 151

Le Clerc, Paul, 164

lesbianism, 148, 149–152

letters. *see* correspondence

Letters of Virginia Woolf Volume Five 1932-1935, 29–30

Levin, Dan and Forrest, 168

lists, use of, 106

Longitude (Sobel), 167

Lovell, Aïda, 31

Lovesong of J. Alfred Prufrock (Eliot), 88

Lyly, *Euphues and his England*, 90

M

male authors, influence of, 88–89

male characters, 153–154

manic depression, 9, 10, 34–35, 35–36, 168

Mann, Thomas, 9

Mansfield, Katherine, 63–64

mathematics, 130

meaning, search for, 134–137

mental illness, 9, 10, 34–35, 35–36, 168

Milton, John, 87

mortality, 112–113, 114–115, 116–117, 121–122, 137

Mother, Great, representations of, 122, 154–155, 156

mother, spiritual, search for, 63–64, 66–67, 156

Mr. Bennett and Mrs. Brown, 82, 92, 143

Mrs. Dalloway, 87, 103–113, 139, 150–154

music, influence of, 97–98, 103–105, 120–121, 120–121
   and mathematics, 130

My Most Favorite Dessert restaurant (Schechter), 164

N

Naiman, Robert, 168

names, of characters, 85

nature, in literary imagery, 71
   and struggle for order, 134–137

Nazi Germany, 3–5, 7, 8, 15–16, 19, 22

New Jersey Federation of Women's Clubs, 22

New York Evening Post, 21–22

New York Herald Tribune, 8, 22–23

New York Public Library, 25, 29–30, 164

New York Times, 20, 22

New York Times Book Review, 168

Nicolson, Harold, *To the New Spirit of Literature*, 117

Nicolson, Nigel, 31–32, 51–52

Night and Day, 78, 86, 96, 127, 143
  comparison with *The Voyage Out*, 68–76

nihilism, and hope, 117–120

O

objectivity, and creativity, 65–66

Oppermanns, The (Feuchtwanger), 9

order, imposing over nature, 134–137

originality vs. tradition, 67, 96–98

Orlando (Woolf), 14–15, 62, 77–83, 87, 89, 90, 90–91, 94–95, 96, 145, 146–147
  gender in, 93, 94, 145–146, 147–148
  time in, 113–114

P

painting, significance of, 122–123

passivity vs. activity, 107–108

Pearl Harbor, 9

Peretz, David, 168

place, in the novel, 111–112, 142-144

Plato, 146

Poe, Edgar Alan, *Ulalume*, 85

Poland, World War II, 6–7, 8

polarity, law of, 124–139

political activism, of women, 155–156, 157–158

Pope, Alexander, 91–92

Pride and Prejudice (Austen), 155–156

Prokosch, Ernst, 10–11

Pseudoxia Epidemica (Browne), 146

"pure have yer", 30–32

R

ratiocination, 72, 109, 127

realism
  vs. emotionalism, 106
  reconciliation with romanticism, 82–83

refugees
  Ethiopian, 168
  World War II, 8–9, 20, 22, 28, 163

Reid, Ogden and Helen Rogers, 8

Relatitatstheorie (Einstein), 114–115

Ribakove-Gordon, Barbara, 167–168

romanticism, 67–68, 70
  vs. classicism, 125–129
  flaws of, 128–129
  reconciliation with realism, 82–83
  satire of, 80–81

room, as setting, 142–144

A Room of One's Own, 14, 63, 66–67, 87, 89, 94, 139–140, 142–143, 145, 157

S

Schechter, Doris, 163
  My Most Favorite Dessert, 164

Schöffler, Herbert, 13, 22, 39

Schuster, Max, 8

Seaman, Barbara, 168

setting, indoor, 142–144

sexual activity, depiction of, 144–145

sexism, 61, 64. *see also* feminism
  room, as refuge from, 142–143
  and social values, 140

sexuality, 144–152
  as fluid concept, 93, 94, 145–146

Shakespeare, William, 66, 86
  King Richard III, 146

Shelley, Percy Bysshe, *Stanzas Written in Dejection Near Naples*, 88

Simon and Schuster Publishers, 8

Smyth, Ethel, 31, 35

Sobel, Dava
  Galileo's Daughter, 167
  Longitude, 167

Soviet Arctic, Gruber writes about, 8

St. Louis (ship), 20

Stalla, Heidi, 28, 167

Stanley, Deborah F., 9

Stanzas Written in Dejection Near Naples (Shelley), 88

State University of New York at Syracuse (SUNY), 9

Stavrogin's Confession (Dostoevsky), 86

Stefansson, Vilhjalmur, 22

Stephen, Leslie, 92

Stevenson, Robert Louis, 87–88

Strachey, Lytton, 2, 92, 93
stream-of-consciousness, 107–108, 111
subjectivity, and creativity, 66
suicide, of Woolf, 9–10, 35–36
Szladits, Lola L., 30
    *Brothers: The Origins of the Henry
    W. and Albert A. Berg Collection
    of English and American Literature,
    The New York Public Library,*
    164–165

T
Tauchnitz Press, Leipzig, 3, 22
time, in the novel, 112–115, 116–117, 125
    one day, 130–131
To the Lighthouse, 90, 114–123, 142,
    154
To the New Spirit of Literature
    (Nicolson), 117
tolerance, of differing styles, 102, 124, 155
tradition vs. originality, 67, 96–98
Turner, Philip, 163, 167
Twain, Mark, *A Connecticut Yankee in
    King Arthur's Court,* 114

U
Ulalume (Poe), 85
Ulysses (Joyce), 91, 95–96
Urn Burial (Browne), 90–91

V
values, social, 140
    feminine, 140–143
Voyage Out, The, 84–85, 86, 124, 132,
    139
    comparison with *Night and Day,*
        68–76

W
The Waves, 10, 17, 88, 124–139, 132,
    140, 141, 155
Webb, Ruth, 30
The Well of Loneliness (Radclyffe
    Hull), 153
West, Margaret, 23–24, 28, 42, 43
window, as literary device, 143–144

Woolf, Leonard, 1–5, 3, 5, 166
    devotion to Virginia, 35, 35–36
    Downhill All the Way, 34
Woolf, Virginia
    anti-Semitism, 35
    correspondence. *see* correspondence
    diaries, 25–26, 31, 32, 34
        and papers, acquisition of,
            165–167
    *Letters of Virginia Woolf Volume
        Five 1932-1935,* 29–30
    mental illness. *see* mental illness; sui-
        cide, of Woolf
    works of. *see Mr. Bennett and Mrs.
        Brown; A Room of One's Own;
        Jacob's Room; Mrs. Dalloway;
        Night and Day;* Orlando; *The
        Common Reader; The Voyage Out;
        The Waves; The Years; To the
        Lighthouse*
Wordsworth, William, 87
World War II Europe, 3–5, 6–7, 8–9,
    12–16, 19
Writers Workshop, 168

Y
Yamaguchi, Liesl, 167
The Years, 27, 33–34

ABOUT THE AUTHOR

Born in Brooklyn, New York in 1911, Ruth Gruber earned her Ph.D. from Cologne University at age twenty, becoming the youngest person in the world to be awarded a doctorate. Her Ph. D. dissertation, "Virginia Woolf: A Study," written in 1931–32, was published in 1935 by the Tauchnitz Press of Leipzig. This seventieth-anniversary edition of the dissertation—the first feminist essay on Woolf—now published as *Virginia Woolf: The Will to Create as a Woman*, marks the first time the book has been published in the United States.

At twenty-three, Gruber became the first journalist to report from the Soviet Arctic, working on a *New York Herald Tribune* series about women under democracy, communism, and fascism. That part of her life is recounted in *Ahead of Time: My Early Years as a Foreign Correspondent*. Harold Ickes, President Roosevelt's secretary of the interior, read Gruber's articles from the Soviet Arctic and in 1940 asked her to study the prospects of Alaska for homesteading G.I.'s after World War II, a period chronicled in the second volume of her memoirs, *Inside of Time: My Journey from Alaska to Israel* (both memoirs are available from Carroll & Graf). In 1944, Ickes asked her to take on another mission: escorting a group of 1,000 Holocaust refugees from Italy to America. She wrote about this experience in *Haven: The Dramatic Story of 1000 WW II Refugees and How they Came to America*, which was also a TV miniseries.

Returning to journalism, Gruber covered the squalid DP camps in Europe, North Africa, and the Middle East, and reported on the founding of Israel, which led to *Destination Palestine*, republished in 1999 as *Exodus 1947: The Ship that Launched a Nation*. Her other books include *Raquela: A Woman of Israel*, winner of the National Jewish Book Award, and *I Went to the Soviet Arctic*.

Gruber has long said that her weapons against injustice, and on behalf of refugees, were her typewriter and her camera. Edward

Steichen urged her to "take pictures with her heart." The photographs have appeared in more than 20 exhibits and documentaries, including the Academy Award-winning documentary, "The Long Way Home."

In 1998 Ruth Gruber received a lifetime achievement award from the American Society of Journalists and Authors. In October 2002, she helped dedicate Safe Haven, a museum in Oswego, New York, dedicated to preserving and learning from the experience of the 1,000 Holocaust survivors she brought to Fort Ontario, a former army camp, in 1944. Gruber lives in New York City and is a popular and compelling lecturer at venues around the country and abroad.

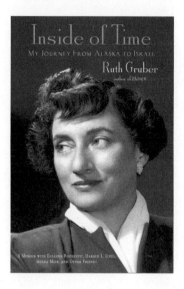